INNER

MIRROR

Work

Find Yourself, Heal Yourself

By

Dr. Christine Edwards, LMHC

Dedication

To the woman in the mirror:
thank you for teaching me that healing begins with honesty,
compassion, and the courage to truly see.

To Jessica Perry:
whose light sparked the practice of mirror work in my life, and
whose inspiration continues to guide my path.

To my loved ones:
for the trials and tribulations that became my teachers, shaping
me into the woman I was always meant to become.

And to every soul who holds this book:
may you stand before your reflection and find not only your
wounds, but also your wholeness, your strength, and your light.

Table of Contents

Introduction:
The Mirror Is Not Your Enemy

There comes a moment in every healing journey when everything goes quiet. The noise fades, the distractions fall away, and the roles you've played so long: the caretaker, the achiever, the fixer, the performer, dissolve into nothingness. You are left utterly alone with yourself.

Facing the raw, unfiltered self takes a level of honesty that feels terrifying, like standing naked in front of a mirror that doesn't lie. To be still is to meet the shadows lurking beneath your carefully crafted mask: the buried shame, the dismissed wounds, and the silenced truths. This confrontation is the turning point where healing becomes real and admits: "I can't keep running. I'm ready to meet myself, every fractured, broken, beautiful part." This truth whispers: You are allowed to be whole. Healing isn't about perfection; it's about showing up for yourself, again and again, with open eyes and an open heart.

Inner Mirror Work is Not Self-Help

This is not simply a self-help book designed to teach you five steps to productivity or a quick-fix path to surface-level happiness. Inner Mirror Work bypasses the pursuit of external coping mechanisms to focus on spiritual and psychological excavation. It's about remembering who you were before trauma, shame, and the weight of expectations crushed your truth. Our goal isn't to look better on the outside; it is to be whole on the inside.

You are Not Alone

Throughout this book, I share pieces of my own story: honest, vulnerable moments from my journey with mirror work. Some are messy, some are tender, but all of them are real. I hope that as you read, you'll not only see my struggles and growth, but also recognize parts of your own story reflected back to you.

These aren't polished or perfect stories. They are real snapshots of my life: moments of struggle, heartbreak, and confusion, but also unexpected breakthroughs. These were times when we confronted parts of ourselves we had long ignored or buried: the heavy shame, the wounds that refused to heal, and the voices we silenced to survive.

I share these reflections not to offer you easy answers or quick fixes, because this work is rarely easy, and healing is never linear. Instead, I share to remind you that you are not walking this path alone. These stories are my way of holding out a hand, saying, "I see you. I understand the weight you carry. And there is a way through."

I hope that by sharing myself in this way, you'll find not only inspiration but also the courage to start, keep going, or go deeper in your own mirror work.

Chapter 1:
What Is Inner Mirror Work?

To engage in this work is to invite a moment of profound recognition. There is a moment, quiet, electric, almost breathless, when you look into your own eyes in the mirror and truly see yourself. Not the version you show the world, not the fixed smile or the polished mask you've learned to wear. But the raw, unfiltered self beneath it all, the part of you that aches to be known, to be healed, and most of all, to be loved.

Carl Jung, a foundational voice in depth psychology, famously said:

"Everything that irritates us about others can lead us to an understanding of ourselves."

That quote lies at the very heart of this practice.

Because what we notice in the world, our triggers, our projections, the pain that shows up in relationships, even the things we project onto others, is often just a mirror of what's happening inside us. It reflects unhealed wounds, the beliefs we've carried from others, and the stories we've come to believe as truth. At its core, Inner Mirror Work rests on a powerful and transformative principle: the external world is not just a backdrop to our existence. It is an active reflection of our inner psychological and emotional landscape. Life isn't simply happening to us. It's happening through us, reflecting back the beliefs, wounds, and energies we carry within.

Think about it. Experiences of rejection, betrayal, invisibility, or chronic misunderstanding in your relationships aren't random acts of cruelty or misfortune. They're mirrors, illuminating the patterns you've internalized: self-neglect, boundary violations, emotional suppression.

Maybe you've caught yourself in this cycle. The same dynamics are playing out on repeat. You give too much. You lash out when you feel unheard. You shrink yourself to fit into spaces that weren't made for you. You chase love that's unavailable or conditional. You feel unseen, again and again.

3

After some time, your mirrors will eventually lead you to a crossroads, a place where you're invited to meet your maker you might not have believed in before. Not a source of rules, judgment, or punishment, but a quiet, steady presence that has been sitting beside your pain all along, waiting patiently for you to stop performing, to drop the act, and simply be.

That is when the real work starts.

That is when you stop just understanding your patterns intellectually and start healing them with courage, compassion, and grace.

Coming Home to Yourself.

My family has always held a negative perception of me, and because of that, I often feel like an outsider in my own story. They believe what others say about me but rarely ask me what really happened. I end up defending myself, explaining myself, and trying to prove my worth in conversations where I should feel most safe. The people who were supposed to show up for me didn't. Over time, I've had to face the painful truth: I am not their priority.

I never felt like I fit in with my family. I was always positioned as the black sheep, and even to this day they continue to cast me as the villain, especially when I try to honor my own needs and set healthy boundaries. I think, in some ways, my reflection back to them, the mirror of my growth and healing, stirs something they don't want to face. Sometimes I wonder if my strength makes them envious because it highlights the parts of themselves they are unwilling to confront. I go out of my way to make them happy in every way I can, yet my efforts are overlooked and never appreciated.

And yet, these same dynamics play out on repeat and not just in my family, but in other relationships too.

I give too much.

I lash out when I feel unheard.

I shrink myself to fit into spaces that weren't meant for me.

I chase love that's unavailable, inconsistent, or conditional.

I feel invisible again and again.

It took me a long time to realize: these patterns are not random.

They are not accidents.

They are messages.

They are *mirrors.*

Each one reflects something within me that still aches to be seen. To be healed. To be reclaimed.

When no one shows up for you, you learn to over-function. You try harder, love louder, and accommodate more. But beneath that effort is a quiet fear that if you don't perform, you'll be left behind. That fear isn't weakness; it's a survival strategy. One that was learned early, repeated often, and embedded deep.

But mirror work teaches us to pause and look at the reflection. Not just at the people who failed us, but at what we began to believe about ourselves in response to that pain. Maybe it's time to ask: *What did I learn to believe about my worth when I wasn't chosen?*

Because the truth is:

You were never unworthy.

You were just surrounded by people who couldn't see clearly.

Their distortion became your internal narrative.

Their neglect became your self-concept.

But it doesn't have to stay that way.

These patterns and these painful echoes are your invitation. They're asking you to stop the cycle. To stop proving. To stop chasing. To stop performing for love that should have been unconditional. They're asking you to meet yourself with the kind of presence and protection no one ever gave you.

This is where the healing begins.

Not by changing others.

But by coming home to yourself.

Mirrors from the Playground

When I was a child, I didn't need to say a word to invite cruelty. My very existence seemed to be enough.

My clothes were barely held together, safety pins where zippers should have been, messy stitches pulling at the seams, ready to rip with one wrong step. My hair tangled, greasy, and unkempt, saying what I couldn't: this child is different. My shoes had already given up, the holes so big my socks pushed through like little white flags of surrender. My clothes were this way not because I didn't care, but because my mother neglected me. She was too busy with her own narcissistic needs to notice that her child was walking through the world exposed and unprotected.

Children notice differences, like sharks notice blood in the water. They circle. They point. They laugh. Their eyes become mirrors that reflect back only what they find wrong. And kids can be merciless when they don't understand poverty or worse, when they do and need someone to feel smaller than themselves.

The teasing wasn't playful. It was calculated in that strange way children are capable of, finding the sorest spot and pressing it over and over. The whispers followed me down hallways like shadows I couldn't escape. The jokes stuck to me like old gum under a desk, ugly, unwanted, and nearly impossible to peel off.

I didn't know the word shame back then. But I knew the sensation: the heat rising in my cheeks, the way my chest felt like it was caving in, the urge to make myself smaller, quieter, invisible. Somewhere inside me, a seed was planted. That seed was a belief that would grow roots so deep it would take years to unearth: *I don't belong. I'm not enough. If people really see me, they'll turn away.*

So, I learned to perform.

I became the chameleon, reading a room before I ever walked into it, adjusting my colors to match what I thought would keep me safe. I overachieved not because I wanted to win, but because I hoped success could hide the parts of me I feared were unlovable. I curated a version of myself that looked strong, capable, untouchable.

Inside, I was still that little girl with safety pins for buttons. I craved connection, but I didn't trust it. Compliments made my skin itch, like they were written for someone else and delivered to me by mistake. Intimacy made me tense, because letting someone in meant giving them a front-row seat to my perceived flaws.

It took years and a thousand tiny moments of self-confrontation to realize something profound: our triggers, our defensiveness, the ruptures that keep repeating in our relationships, they are not random. They are mirrors. They reflect the wounds we never healed, the stories we never meant to adopt but carry anyway.

When I felt unseen in a relationship, it wasn't just about the other person's neglect; it was because of the little girl inside me, the one who once stood alone on the playground, pretending she didn't care about being left out. When I reacted harshly, it wasn't always about the present argument; it was the reflex of a child who had learned that hiding behind armor felt safer than being open.

Healing didn't arrive in some big, dramatic moment. It came slowly, through small acts of courage. It came when I allowed myself to look back at that little girl, not with the shame the world once showed her, but with the kindness she always deserved. Her patched clothes and worn-out shoes weren't signs of failure, but proof of her strength and survival.

She was never the problem.

Today, she no longer has to earn her place in a room. She no longer has to contort herself to be acceptable. She is loved, not for the version she learned to perform, but for the person she always was.

Psychology asks:

What happened to me, and how did it shape me?

Spirituality asks:

What parts of me got lost in that shaping, and how do I bring them home?

Psychology can help you understand.

But spirituality helps you *unhook*.

You can do years of talk therapy and still feel stuck. Not because you're broken, but because you haven't *invited a deeper source of healing into the pattern.*

You haven't asked:

What sacred truth is being blocked by this belief?

What part of me is still operating from a wound instead of wisdom?

The mind can trace the story.

The soul is what rewrites it.

What Unhooked Me

I lost the part of me that believed I was allowed to take up space.

The part that didn't flinch at the sound of footsteps.

The part that laughed too loud, made messes, asked questions, and didn't apologize for simply existing.

I lost the softness and the innocent belief that I was lovable without proving it, without performing perfection, without earning safety by staying small.

I lost trust in my own feelings. I learned to scan every room, every face, for signs of danger or disappointment. I became the peacekeeper, the perfectionist, the hyper-aware child who took on the emotional weight of the adults around me, because if I could just be good enough, maybe the chaos would stop.

In that shaping, I became what the moment demanded. But I lost what my soul needed.

And bringing those lost parts home does not happen all at once.

It happens in whispers.

In the moments I stop trying to justify my emotions.

These days, I let myself rest, even when the dishes aren't done.

In the mirror, when I look at my reflection and don't wince or critique, but simply see.

It happens every time I tell the scared parts of me: You didn't deserve that. It wasn't your fault. And you are safe now.

Bringing myself home means letting that little girl cry without rushing her to be strong.

It means letting the woman I am now choose softness without fear of punishment.

It means reclaiming joy, pleasure, and freedom, not as indulgences, but as birthrights.

This is the work of healing.

Not becoming someone new.

But returning to the self I was always meant to be.

Whole. Worthy. Home.

Beyond the Glass: Mirrors in Daily Life

Mirror work extends far beyond the literal mirror on your wall. It lives in your daily experiences, your relationships, your reactions, your emotions. Every time you feel triggered, dismissed, unseen, overly sensitive, or deeply irritated, life is offering you a mirror. Not to shame you, but to awaken you. These moments aren't just random feelings; they are signals, showing you where your inner healing or growth is needed.

Each interaction becomes an invitation to turn inward. When someone doesn't listen to you, it may echo a time when your voice was not heard. When you feel jealousy rising, it might point to a forgotten desire within you that longs for expression. When you're deeply affected by someone's behavior, ask: *What part of me is being touched right now?* Is it fear? Abandonment? Neglect? Abuse? The need for control? The ache for validation?

In this way, the world becomes a living mirror, a stage where your inner wounds, unmet needs, and untended desires play out. Your boss may reflect your inner critic. Your partner may mirror your need for safety. Your friend's distance may awaken an old fear of being left behind. None of these are punishments; they are prompts. They call you not to react blindly, but to respond consciously.

When you begin to view life this way, you stop looking outside of yourself for all the answers. You realize that healing doesn't just happen in therapy or meditation, it happens in the grocery store line, in difficult conversations, in the quiet moment of loneliness, in your morning commute. Every experience is feedback. Every moment holds a message.

The real mirror isn't the glass in your bathroom or your reflection in a store window; it's how you face life, especially the moments that make you uncomfortable. Those moments are your greatest teachers. And if you're willing to look not just at *what* happened but *why* it affects you so deeply, you'll begin to see yourself more clearly than any mirror ever could.

"What you meet in another being is the projection of your own level of evolution."
— *Ram Dass*

The Day I Started Questioning Everything

For most of my life, I lived by a set of invisible rules I didn't remember choosing but followed as if my survival depended on them.

I believed I had to be perfect to be worthy: perfect grades, perfect behavior, perfect appearance, and perfect career. Every mistake felt like a public crack in the image I had worked so hard to maintain. I believed that vulnerability was a liability, an opening for people to judge me, hurt me, or leave. I believed that my value was determined entirely by other people's opinions, by their nods of approval, their smiles of acceptance, their silence when I got it 'right.'

My father once told me I was never going to amount to anything, and that when I made as much money as him, I could call the shots. Until then, my thoughts and feelings meant nothing. Even when I succeeded in my career, my achievements were overlooked and minimized, as if they carried no value at all. His words etched themselves into my self-image, making me feel as though no matter how hard I worked, it would never be enough.

These weren't truths I had decided for myself. They were stories passed down to me, shaped by my family's expectations, the culture I grew up in, and the quiet, unspoken rules of my home. My mother's sharp words when I didn't measure up, the praise that only came when I did exceptionally well, the disapproving looks when I showed too much emotion, these were my early lessons. I absorbed them like oxygen, too young to know I could choose a different air to breathe.

But perfection is a heavy costume to wear. Over time, it began to crush me.

I remember sitting at my desk late one night, surrounded by work I couldn't seem to finish, my chest tight with anxiety. I had just gotten off the phone with a close friend after a disagreement, and instead of feeling safe enough to explain my feelings, I had defaulted to my usual role: calm, agreeable, "fine." When I hung up, a hollow ache set in. I realized I had been performing again, not just with them, but everywhere. Even with myself.

It wasn't a dramatic breakdown. No shouting, no sobbing on the floor. Just a quiet, disorienting recognition: most of the beliefs I'd been clinging to weren't mine. They were hand-me-downs, sewn together from other people's wounds, fears, and limitations. And I had been wearing them as if they were my own skin.

For the first time, I asked myself questions I had avoided for years:

What if I don't have to earn love by being perfect?

What if my worth has nothing to do with other people's approval?

What if the very vulnerability I've been hiding is actually my strength?

Those questions felt dangerous, like pulling at a thread I wasn't sure I could stop unraveling. But beneath the fear was something else: a spark. A tiny, stubborn hope that I could write a different story for myself.

So I began, slowly, to challenge the rules. I let myself show up to a gathering without over-rehearsing every conversation. I admitted to a friend that I was struggling instead of brushing it off. I left an email unpolished and sent it anyway. And to my surprise, the world didn't fall apart. In some ways, it opened up.

It wasn't easy. Some days, the old patterns roared back louder than ever, convincing me to retreat into my polished shell. And sometimes I did. But each time I stepped out again, each time I allowed my imperfections to be seen and still found myself accepted, I loosened the grip of those inherited beliefs just a little more.

It has been messy, sometimes painful work. I've had to grieve the years I spent disconnecting from my own truth. But the more I lean into authenticity, the lighter I feel. I've learned that I can be imperfect and still be whole. I can be vulnerable and still be strong. I can be loved, not for the image I project, but for the person I actually am.

That night, sitting at my desk in the quiet, I didn't know it yet, but I had taken the first step toward living my own story. One did not define by fear, performance, or impossible standards, but by the courage to belong to myself.

Themes Often Revealed Through Mirror Work

- Childhood wounds and unmet emotional needs
- Repetitive relationship patterns
- Limiting beliefs around worth, love, and success
- Emotional triggers and suppressed feelings
- Generational shame, abandonment, or guilt

"If you do not bring forth what is within you, what you do not bring forth will destroy you."
— *The Gospel of Thomas*

The Practice

When doing this work you enter into a sacred covenant with yourself, a vow to stop abandoning your inner truth and start meeting it with honesty, grace, and courage. It is a practice of seeing, not just with your eyes, but with your heart. You shift from autopilot to awareness. You become the *witness* to your inner world, not the judge. Curious instead of critical. Compassionate rather than condemning.

It isn't always easy. Some days, it can feel uncomfortable, even painful. You may see and feel parts of yourself you've hidden for years: the version of you that still feels small, scared, or unworthy. The anger you suppressed. The grief you never voiced. The masks you've worn to survive. But each time you choose to stay, to breathe, to listen, you are healing.

The Voice That Questions Everything

Family was supposed to be my first safe place.

It wasn't.

In our house, love and fear lived in the same room. My mother's anger could arrive without warning, a slammed cupboard, a sharp inhale, her footsteps coming faster than my mind could prepare. I learned to read the air the way some kids read storybooks: Was the room too quiet? Was her jaw tight? Was the way she set down her coffee cup just a little too hard? These were the signals that determined whether the day would be peaceful or stormy.

My father's silence didn't soothe; it suffocated. He was there, but not *present*, disappearing into his own world when we needed him to anchor ours. When my mother's anger exploded, he would disappear into the garage or sink into his chair, staring at the TV without really watching it. From that, I learned something dangerous: when life gets hard, people leave, even if they're still in the room and their bodies stay.

The rules in our family were clear, though no one ever said them out loud:

Don't speak unless spoken to.

Don't make mistakes.

Don't expect comfort.

I learned early that emotions were liabilities. If I cried, it was "too much." If I was hurt, I was "too sensitive." If I got angry, I was "just like her," and I wanted nothing less than to be like her. So, I swallowed it all. The sadness. The fear. The shame. I locked them away so tightly that I even forgot where I put them.

But trauma doesn't vanish just because you refuse to look at it. It hides in your reflexes, in the way you flinch at sudden movements, in the way you over-explain when you make a small mistake, in the way you brace for someone's disappointment before it even comes. It creeps into your relationships, convincing you to choose partners who feel familiar, even if familiar means unsafe.

For years, I told myself it was just the past. That I had moved on. What happened back then has no power over me now. But every time I found myself apologizing for simply existing, every time I felt that old fear knotting in my stomach, I knew the truth: my body remembered. My heart remembered.

Healing has meant going back to that house in my mind, not to stay, but to see it clearly. To acknowledge the chaos, I grew up in without making it my home anymore. To grieve the parents, I needed and didn't get. To understand that their pain wasn't my fault, and it's not my responsibility to carry it.

Family trauma does leave scars, but it also creates space for new things to grow, like compassion, healthy boundaries, and self-trust. Now, when I feel that familiar fear rising, I remind myself: I am not that child anymore. I can step out of the storm. I can choose my own weather.

Ask yourself questions that reach beneath the surface:

What am I believing about myself at this moment?

Whose voice is speaking in my head, and is it even mine?

What truth have I been afraid to face, and what would happen if I met it with love?

It is a process of learning and unlearning. You begin to strip away the layers of conditioning that told you who you *should* be and instead reconnect with who you *truly* are. You reclaim lost parts of yourself, not to fix them, but to embrace them. Every crack, every scar, every shadow becomes part of the mosaic of your wholeness.

And with time, something beautiful happens. You stop reacting blindly. You stop being ruled by old stories or outdated wounds.

Instead, you respond with clarity and intention. You become more anchored, more present, more sovereign in your own life. You return to yourself, not as a version someone else created, but as your most honest, integrated self.

That is the heart of the practice. Not perfection. Not performance. But presence.

And through that presence, you become your own source of safety, truth, and love.

The Mirror and the Turning Point

For years, I looked in the mirror just long enough to ensure my mask was in place: a mask of being "fine," of managing everything. I avoided looking deeper, afraid of seeing the truth: the exhaustion, the tension, and the smallness I had adopted while navigating life with my ex-husband's alcoholism.

One morning, that changed. I stopped scanning for flaws; instead, I simply stared. I saw the weight I had been carrying, the bracing posture born from years of trying to control the unpredictable, trying to be perfect enough to earn safety or stability. I realized I was avoiding my own reflection because I was afraid of seeing the self that had been surviving, the part of me tired of always having to be the strong, capable one.

I started asking better questions:

- "What am I carrying that no one else sees?"
- "What part of me is begging not to be fixed, but to be held?"

The mirror stopped being a judge and became a portal. It led not into who I was supposed to be, but into the self that had been waiting beneath the survival tactics and the perfectionism.

Today, I still see the lines and tired eyes, but I also see someone who survived and who is standing without shrinking. I am learning to replace the voices that said I wasn't enough with my own voice of self-acceptance.

Transforming Mistakes into Wisdom

What if you let go of the heavy burden and shame connected to the relationship, and instead saw that difficult chapter as a sacred journey?

The experiences you went through, the pain, the confusion, the betrayal, were not punishments. Their lessons were not meant to break you, but to wake you up. This is a shift from guilt to growth, from shame to self-awareness.

Think of the painful experiences from that marriage:

- The betrayal that taught you the absolute necessity of setting boundaries.
- The heartbreak that revealed the depth of love you have to give and where you truly deserve to place it.
- The time you abandoned yourself for the sake of the relationship, only to learn that your own voice and self-worth matter most.

These aren't just scars; they are symbols of initiation. They asked you to grow, to become braver, and more aligned with who you truly are. You can stop obsessing over what you could have done differently and begin to ask, "What strength did this reveal in me that I didn't know I had?"

You are not the sum of your so-called mistakes in that relationship. You are the person who walked through them.

That makes you powerful. That makes you wise. That makes you whole.

"Try not to resist the changes that come your way. Instead, let life live through you."

— Rumi

The Day I Chose Life

Being caught in addiction wasn't just about the substance itself; it was a relentless series of trials and tribulations that tested every part of me.

There were the physical battles first, the endless exhaustion, the shakes that sometimes came unbidden, the sleepless nights when my mind raced and my body screamed for relief. Every day, I wrestled with cravings that felt like a storm inside my chest, an itch that couldn't be scratched no matter how much I tried to push it away. The hangovers weren't physical symptoms; they were a deep, gnawing despair that left me feeling broken and hollow before the day had even begun.

Then came the emotional toll. Addiction pulled me into a labyrinth of shame and guilt so thick it was hard to breathe. I lied to friends, to family, to myself, trying to cover the cracks with stories and excuses. Each lie piled on top of the last until I barely recognized the person I saw in the mirror. I became a stranger in my own life, disconnected from my feelings, from my hopes, from the people who once mattered most.

Relationships crumbled under the weight of my addiction. Trust, once broken, was hard to rebuild. I pushed away those who tried to help, sometimes out of pride, sometimes out of fear they'd see the real me, the one I was desperately trying to hide. Loneliness crept in, not just from isolation, but from the isolation within myself. It was a loneliness wrapped in self-loathing, a constant companion that reminded me of my failures.

Financial struggles piled up, too. Money I didn't have disappeared chasing the next high, bills went unpaid, and opportunities slipped away because addiction's grip distorted my priorities. I found myself caught in a cycle of desperation, needing to feed the addiction but knowing each choice pulled me further from the life I wanted.

There were moments of near ruin, brushes with legal trouble, health scares that shook me to my core, and nights spent in fear of what might come next. Yet, even when hitting rock bottom seemed inevitable, the addiction whispered that I was fine, that I could handle it, that tomorrow would be better.

And through it all, I battled internally, the part of me that still hoped for healing, still dreamed of freedom, still wanted to believe in a better version of myself. But hope felt fragile and distant, often overshadowed by the weight of the day-to-day struggle.

Then, one quiet morning, I paused, taking a moment just for myself, no distractions, no defenses. I looked inward, noticing the pain and exhaustion that had quietly settled over me. I asked the questions I'd been too afraid to voice, the ones I had long avoided: the truths I needed to confront to begin truly seeing myself.

What am I carrying that no one sees? Whose voice lives rent-free in my mind? What part of me is begging not to be fixed, but to be held?

The mirror didn't lie. It showed me the layers beneath the addiction: the fear, the grief, the longing for connection and peace.

It forced me to confront not just the surface struggles but the deeper wounds I'd been running from.

That moment of mirror work became a turning point. It didn't erase the hardships, but it gave me a space to begin healing, to start loving the fractured, messy person staring back at me. To recognize that surviving the trials of addiction was not the end, but the beginning of reclaiming my life and my self-worth.

Reflection Questions: Begin Your Journey

1. What situations in my daily life consistently trigger me, and what deeper belief or wound might those triggers be pointing to?

   _____

   _____

   _____

   _____

   _____

   _____

   _____

   _____

   _____

   _____

2. What patterns do I keep repeating in my relationships, and what might they be reflecting about how I see myself?

   _____

   _____

   _____

   _____

   _____

_____

_____

_____

_____

_____

3. Which patterns in my life feel cyclical or unresolved? What might they be mirroring back to me?

_____

_____

_____

_____

_____

_____

_____

_____

4. What do I admire in others, and how might that be a reflection of something within me I've disowned or not yet claimed?

_____

_____

_____

_____

_____

_____

_____

_____

_____

5.   What do I judge harshly in others, and could that judgment
     be pointing to something unresolved within myself?

_____

_____

_____

_____

_____

_____

_____

_____

6.   When I feel rejected, abandoned, or criticized, what story
     do I tell myself—and where did that story begin?

_____

_____

_____

_____

_____

_____

_____

7. What part of me have I tried to hide or suppress in order to be accepted?

What emotion do I most avoid feeling, and what would happen if I allowed myself to feel it fully?

_____

_____

_____

_____

_____

_____

_____

_____

8. What "mask" do I wear in certain environments (e.g., the helper, the achiever, the peacemaker), and what am I protecting underneath that mask?

_____

_____

_____

_____

_____

_____

_____

_____

Chapter 2:
The Power and Purpose of Self-Reflection -
Where Psychology Meets Spirit

"Know thyself and thou shalt know the universe and the gods."
— Socrates

The journey of coming home to the self begins with a commitment to seeing clearly. This practice, which Socrates famously called knowing thyself, is more than just a way to grow; it's an act of quiet rebellion in today's fast, noisy world. In a society where endless scrolling has replaced silence and performance often matters more than being present, taking time to look within is a sacred way to reclaim your true self. Self-reflection is the very bedrock of inner transformation

Sitting In Silence

I still remember the time I truly sat in silence, with no phone in my hand, no to-do list scattered nearby, just me, my thoughts, and a mirror. It wasn't planned or scheduled; it just happened one day when exhaustion caught up with me, and I found myself alone in a quiet room with nowhere to run. At first, the stillness felt like a weight pressing down on my chest. I wanted to fill the space with noise or distraction, but something inside whispered that I couldn't I had to face it.

What started as a simple pause quickly became a reckoning.

In that silence, the mirror reflected more than just my physical image. It magnified everything I'd spent years avoiding the doubts that whispered I wasn't enough, the inherited beliefs passed down like unspoken rules from generations before me, and the stories I had wrapped around myself like a second skin to protect against a world that felt unkind.

And it showed me the ache beneath those reflections was the ache of relationships that fell apart, not for lack of trying, but because the expectations I had carried were never met. I saw the disappointment etched deep in my eyes: the partners who promised they would love me and show up for me but instead kept me at a distance, the friendships that faded when I needed them most, the silent goodbyes after too many misunderstandings. Each broken connection left a wound I tried to hide, but the mirror didn't let me look away.

I saw the fear behind my eyes, the exhaustion in my posture, and the cracks in the armor I'd built to hide vulnerability.

It was uncomfortable, even painful, to face those truths so plainly. In that discomfort, I found an unexpected clarity. I saw that I had been living in fragments, only showing the parts I thought were safe; while hiding the ones I feared others would reject. To heal, I realized, wasn't about just putting those pieces together. It meant truly knowing myself, not the polished version I showed the world, but the whole of me, with my flaws, fears, and hopes included.

That moment was the beginning of a journey, a commitment to meet myself fully, with curiosity instead of judgment, with kindness instead of shame. It meant sitting with the hard questions: Who am I beneath the surface? What parts of me have I neglected or denied? What wounds am I still carrying that need to be seen and healed?

Sitting in front of that mirror taught me that healing isn't about perfection or quick fixes. It's about presence and showing up for yourself every day, even when it's hard, even when you don't have all the answers. It's about slowly peeling back the layers until what's left is raw and real.

And in that rawness, I found something precious: the beginning of self-acceptance, the foundation for true growth, and the courage to embrace the fullness of who I am, despite the disappointments, despite the broken relationships, despite the unmet expectations.

Self-reflection is the bedrock of transformation. It is not passive pondering or overthinking. It's the intentional, soul-deep process of excavating the internal architecture of your life, including your values, conditioning, wounds, and truths.

"Owning our story and loving ourselves through that process is the bravest thing that we'll ever do."

— Brené Brown

To reflect deeply is not simply to think; it is to *remember*, *reclaim*, and *re-see* ourselves with kindness and empathy.

It is an act of inner excavation, a return to the self beneath the noise, beneath the masks, beneath the protective walls we've built to survive.

Reflection is how we meet the truth of our experience, not as critics, but as curious witnesses.

It's not about obsessing over the past or judging ourselves for how we showed up.

It's about pausing long enough to ask: *What story have I been living? And is it still true?*

To reflect is to peel back the layers:

- The mask of perfection we wear to be accepted.
- The roles we perform to feel loved, successful, or worthy.
- The habits and patterns we repeat not because they serve us, but because they're familiar.
- The emotions we've buried - grief, rage, longing, fear - just to keep moving forward in a world that rarely pauses to ask *how we're really doing.*

And beneath all of that? You.

The *real* you. The version of you before the disappointments, before the labels, before the world told you who you should be.

The version that still exists, quietly, patiently, beneath the armor.

The you that longs not for perfection, but for *presence.*

"Between stimulus and response, there is a space. In that space is our power to choose our response. In our response lies our growth and our freedom."

— Viktor E. Frankl

That space is what reflection gives us back.

It interrupts the autopilot. It widens the gap between the trigger and the reaction.

It's the breath before the decision. The stillness before the shift.

And it is in that sacred pause that we get to choose, consciously, who we want to be next.

Reflection helps us reclaim agency.

It is how we move from being *shaped by life* to *shaping our life.*

It helps us ask bigger questions:

- What values am I living by?
- Whose expectations am I still trying to meet?
- What parts of me have I silenced in order to be safe?

To reflect is to take radical responsibility, not to blame ourselves, but to honor ourselves enough to grow.

It is how we harvest wisdom from our pain.

How we find patterns in our chaos.

How we stop reacting from the past and begin responding from the present.

Reflection doesn't always lead to immediate answers, but it always leads to deeper awareness. And from that awareness, all healing begins.

So, take the time.

Pause.

Feel.

Ask.

Listen.

Because when you reflect deeply, you don't just look at your life.

You *see yourself*, maybe for the first time.

To reflect is also to return to Source. Beneath the masks and mechanisms, the striving and shame, there is a soul that remembers. Reflection is not only psychological; it is spiritual. It serves as the soul's gentle way of knocking on the door of our awareness, reminding us that we are more than our wounds and roles. In the silence of reflection, we meet the Divine not as something outside of us, but as the quiet, enduring presence within us. That sacred pause becomes a sanctuary, a place where God can speak, where grace can enter, and where our fragmented selves begin to reunite. Reflection is not just healing; it is holy.

"Search me, O God, and know my heart; test me and know my anxious thoughts. See if there is any offensive way in me and lead me in the way everlasting."

— Psalm 139:23 – 24

"Do not dwell in the past, do not dream of the future, concentrate the mind on the present moment."

— The Buddha

The Moment the Mask Fell

For years, I believed my masks were my superpower. The practiced smile that hid my trembling heart. The quick laugh that disguised the ache beneath. The endless busyness that drowned out the silence I feared. Those masks were my armor, my carefully crafted shield against a world that felt too raw, too unpredictable.

But one afternoon, everything changed in a way I never saw coming.

I sat there, eyes glued to the screen, nodding as if I was fully engaged. On the outside, I looked composed, maybe even strong. But inside, a hurricane of anxiety, self-doubt, and exhaustion was tearing me apart. Then came a simple question, one so ordinary that it should have been easy to answer. But at that moment, my mask cracked.

My voice shook. My defenses crumbled. I was exposed, unfiltered, unguarded, utterly vulnerable.

It was terrifying. And yet, somehow, it was the first breath of freedom I'd taken in a long time.

In that raw, unguarded moment, I finally saw what all the pretending had cost me. The energy wasted, the parts of myself buried deep, the desperate longing to be truly seen and accepted— not for the version I polished and performed, but for the real me.

Since then, I've been on a slow, often messy journey of peeling back those layers. The masks don't come off all at once. Old habits cling like shadows. But with every small step, I've discovered something remarkable: vulnerability isn't weakness, it's the gateway to connection, healing, and genuine strength.

Beneath the masks and mechanisms lies a truth waiting to be lived. And when you dare to show up fully, messily, imperfectly, and authentically, life shifts in ways you never imagined.

The Aims of Inner Reflection Through Spirit:

- To foster profound self-awareness
- To expose unconscious patterns and core wounds

- To reconnect with the inner child, intuition, and authentic self
- To rewrite outdated stories and birth new, empowered narratives

Self-awareness is more than knowing your favorite foods or recognizing what annoys you. It's not just about being able to say, *"I'm a morning person"* or *"I get frustrated when plans change."* True self-awareness digs deeper than personality quirks and preferences. It asks *why*.

Why does your chest tighten when someone raises their voice?

Why do you find it hard to maintain eye contact when you're feeling vulnerable?

Why does your mood shift suddenly in certain environments?

The answers to those questions aren't always easy to find. They often live in the shadowy corners of our memories, buried in childhood patterns, trauma responses, or internalized beliefs about who we are *allowed* to be.

To deepen your self-awareness is to become an observer of your inner landscape. It's about noticing what rises up within you, without immediately reacting or judging. It's sitting with discomfort long enough to hear what it wants to teach you.

Because every reaction has a root, every shutdown has a story.

You might notice that you shut down when emotions rise, not because you're cold or indifferent, but because somewhere deep inside, you learned that shutting down was safe. Maybe your feelings were dismissed or punished. Maybe you were taught that expressing emotion made you weak or unlovable. Over time, silence became your armor. Distance became your protector.

But here's the hard truth:

You can't heal what you're still running from, even if the escape is only in your mind.

Avoidance shows up in many ways, like distraction, overworking, people-pleasing, perfectionism, or even spiritual bypassing. The moment something gets too close to our pain, we pull back. We intellectualize instead of feeling. We smile instead of crying. We explain instead of expressing ourselves.

Healing begins when we stop running and start listening.

When you deepen your self-awareness, you begin to reclaim parts of yourself that have long been exiled. You learn to recognize the voice of your inner critic and to question whether it tells the truth. You begin to notice your automatic reactions and ask, *Is this habit keeping me safe, or keeping me stuck?* You begin to see the gap between who you've become and who you truly are beneath the conditioning.

Self-awareness is a form of sacred rebellion.

It's the courageous act of turning inward, especially when the world says to keep performing, producing, and pleasing. It's choosing to become intimate with your truth, even when it's messy, especially when it's messy.

Sometimes awareness comes with grief, grief for all the years spent disconnected, all the times you betrayed your own need to stay accepted, all the love you didn't know how to receive. But grief is not the enemy. It's the doorway back to yourself.

To deepen self-awareness is to understand that your patterns are not personal failings; they are survival strategies. And they made sense once. But you are not living *then* anymore. You are here now. And here, you get to choose differently.

Here, you get to pause instead of react.

You get to speak instead of shutting down.

You get to feel instead of fleeing.

You get to become who you were before the world told you to be someone else.

My Story of Losing My Dad

Losing my dad brought a flood of emotions I wasn't fully prepared to face. For years, he had been distant, physically absent from many parts of my life, emotionally detached, and often critical when he was around. The relationship wasn't one of warmth or closeness; instead, it was marked by a quiet tension, unspoken disappointment, and a persistent feeling that I was never quite enough for him.

When he passed away, I expected to feel relief, or at least a calm closure. Instead, I was met with confusion and a swirling storm inside me. How do you grieve someone who was so distant? Someone whose presence often felt like an absence. I realized that grief isn't just for the people we loved unconditionally or who loved us back openly. It is also for the unmet needs, the longing for connection, and the hurt from unresolved wounds.

There was a deep sadness for the father I wished I had, the father who could have been there to celebrate my victories or comfort me in my failures. But there was also anger, frustration, and even guilt. Why did I want him to be different? Why did his criticism sting so much? And why did I sometimes wish he had never been part of my life at all?

Through this grief, I began to see more clearly how his distance shaped who I am, my fears of rejection, my desire for approval, and my struggles to feel worthy. I started to understand that mourning him wasn't just about his death; it was about mourning the relationship that never fully existed, and the child in me who still longs for a father's acceptance.

Grief became a bridge to self-awareness. It helped me recognize my patterns and emotional scars, but it also opened space for compassion and for him, for myself, and for the complexity of human relationships. It taught me that it's okay to hold conflicting feelings: love and hurt, longing and anger, grief and relief.

Losing my dad wasn't the end of my story; it was a chapter in my ongoing journey of healing, growth, and learning to find peace within myself, even when the past remains unresolved.

Real-Life Moments:

You dread Sundays, and for a while, you couldn't quite put your finger on why.

It's the one-day others often associate with peace, rest, or spiritual renewal. But for you, it feels different.

Heavier. Tighter in the chest.

The morning feels quietly loaded. The pressure builds before you've even opened your eyes.

And then, through reflection, it becomes clear:

Sundays used to mean church. And the church didn't feel safe.

Maybe it was the pressure to dress a certain way, speak a certain way, believe a certain way.

Perhaps it was the forced smiles that hid deep sadness or shame.

Maybe it was the silence around real issues, the fear of judgment, or the subtle message that parts of you were "wrong" or "unworthy."

Maybe it was religious trauma masked as righteousness, sermons that shamed instead of healed, leaders who manipulated instead of guided.

Your body remembers what your mind tried to suppress.

The feeling of being watched. The expectation to show faith instead of truly experiencing it. The loneliness of sitting in a pew and feeling invisible.

The contradiction of being told God is love, but only if you fit the mold.

And so now, as Sundays come around, your nervous system flinches, not out of rebellion, but out of *memory*.

You brace yourself without knowing why.

You feel uneasy during times others call holy.

You're not broken for that, you're *remembering*.

This is the work of deep reflection: not just noticing what you feel but asking *why*.

It's the act of connecting the emotional dots between your past and your present.

It's understanding that your resistance isn't laziness or bitterness, it's a signal. It's the part of you that once sat quietly in shame, finally speaking up.

And now that you see it, you can choose to respond differently.

You can grieve the version of you who didn't have words for what felt wrong.

You can begin to redefine what sacred means to you.

Maybe now, the sacred looks like solitude. Like journaling instead of sermons.

Maybe it looks like walking barefoot in the grass. Listening to your own breath.

Maybe it means talking to the Divine in your own language and not the one that was handed to you, but the one that feels like home.

Sundays don't have to stay heavy.

You get to reclaim them.

You get to create new meaning, grounded in authenticity rather than obligation.

You get to build a relationship with spirituality or silence that is based on freedom, not fear.

This is how healing begins.

Not by erasing the past, but by honoring it and choosing something gentler for your future.

The Yes That Cost You: Meeting the Part That Couldn't Say No

You say *yes* to everything.

To every request, every favor, every invitation, even when your body says no.

You smile. You agree. You show up.

And then later, in the quiet, the resentment creeps in.

You feel drained, frustrated, and unappreciated. You wonder why no one seems to consider your needs, why you're always the giver, the helper, the one others count on, even when you're running on empty.

But in mirror work, you go deeper.

You look beyond the present moment, beyond the calendar full of obligations and the aching fatigue.

And you meet a younger version of yourself, the one who learned that *no* was dangerous.

That *did not lead* to silence. To withdraw. To punish.

To be left out, talked about, made to feel guilty.

You meet the child who realized early on that being agreeable meant staying safe. That being helpful meant being loved.

That pleasing others, even at the cost of herself, was the only way to belong.

And suddenly, it all makes sense.

You didn't become a people-pleaser by accident.

You became one out of necessity.

Your nervous system equated *yes* with connection.

And *not with* abandonment.

So of course, you said yes. You needed to feel needed.

Because if they needed you, maybe they wouldn't leave.

If you kept the peace, maybe you wouldn't feel the pain of conflict or rejection.

But now, through reflection, you begin to understand that the resentment you feel isn't a flaw; it's a message.

A signal that your boundaries are being crossed, and often by your own doing.

A quiet scream from the self you've been silencing to keep others comfortable.

And in this moment, in front of your inner mirror, you don't scold yourself.

You don't shame the version of you who said yes too often.

Instead, you *thank* yourself.

You protected yourself. You've gotten through situations where you didn't have the power to say no.

You helped yourself survive.

But now you're not surviving, you're awakening.

And with that awakening comes choice.

You begin practicing the sacred pause.

You learn to check in with your body before answering.

You experiment with small no's, noticing how the world doesn't fall apart when you honor your truth.

You grieve the friendships that may shift. You mourn the identity that was tied to being "the reliable one."

And you begin to build something new: a self that is whole, not hollow.

Because real love, a real connection, doesn't require self-abandonment.

It allows room for *honest boundaries*.

And in reclaiming your no, you also reclaim your yes.

A yes, that's rooted in desire, not obligation.

A yes that gives, but doesn't drain.

A yes that comes from fullness, not fear.

This is the alchemy of mirror work:

You see the truth, hold it gently, and choose differently.

Not because you're broken, but because you're finally ready to stop betraying yourself in the name of belonging.

The Cost of Saying Yes

For as long as I can remember, saying "yes" felt like the easiest way to keep the peace. Whether it was agreeing to plans when I wanted to stay home, taking on extra tasks at work even when I was overwhelmed, or smoothing over conflicts by swallowing my own needs. I was a people pleaser through and through.

At first, it seemed harmless, even noble. I thought if I made others happy, I'd be liked, valued, and safe. But slowly, I started to feel the weight of it all. Saying yes to everyone else meant saying no to myself. I became exhausted, anxious, and sometimes resentful, feelings I buried deep because I didn't want to seem difficult or ungrateful.

One day, I realized that in trying so hard to please others, I had lost touch with who I really was. My boundaries had disappeared, and my voice felt faint, like a whisper no one could hear. I wasn't living for me anymore; I was living for everyone else's approval.

Changing that wasn't easy. Saying "no" felt uncomfortable, even wrong. But with time, I learned that setting boundaries isn't selfish; it's necessary. People pleasing had cost me my peace and my authenticity, but letting go of it has given me back my freedom.

Now, when I feel the urge to say "yes" out of obligation or fear, I pause and ask myself: *Is this coming from my true self or my need to please?* It's not perfect, and I still stumble, but each time I choose myself, I grow stronger, clearer, and more at peace.

1. What am I feeling right now, and can I name it without judgment?
2. What part of me have I been hiding or silencing out of fear?
3. Where in my life am I pretending to be okay when I'm not?
4. What do I need most from myself today, emotionally, spiritually, or physically?
5. When was the last time I truly felt proud of who I am becoming?
6. What is one truth about me I've been afraid to face but know deep down?

7. Whose approval am I still chasing, and what would happen if I stopped?

8. What does my inner voice sound like? Am I speaking to myself with kindness or criticism?

9. What do I believe I have to do or be in order to be lovable or worthy?

10. What recurring pattern in my life is trying to teach me something I haven't yet learned?

1. **"When I feel emotionally overwhelmed, my first instinct is to..."**

    Explore what you tend to do, shut down, lash out, distract yourself, and where that response might come from

2. **"I notice my body feels tense when..."**

    Pay attention to physical sensations as messengers. What is your body trying to tell you?

3. **"One memory that shaped how I handle conflict is..."**

    Write freely about an experience that influenced the way you respond in emotionally charged situations.

4. **"A part of myself I've been avoiding is..."**

    Be honest: is there an emotion, habit, or truth you've been keeping in the shadows?

5. **"What I needed to hear as a child, but didn't, was..."**

    Speak to your younger self. This is a powerful way to reconnect with unmet emotional needs.

6. **"I protect myself by..."**

    What behaviors do you use as defense mechanisms? How do they serve you, and how might they also limit you?

7. **"The story I often tell myself about who I am is..."**

    Reflect on the narrative you carry. Is it empowering or limiting? Where did it come from?

8. **"I know I'm disconnected from myself when..."**

    What are the signs that you're out of alignment, emotionally, physically, or spiritually?

9. **"A pattern I keep repeating is..."**

> What situations do you find yourself in again and again? What might be beneath that repetition?

10. **"I am learning that it's safe to..."**

> Complete this with something you're ready to begin trusting yourself with, such as feeling, expressing, asking for, and receiving.

II. Uncovering Unconscious Habits and Assumptions

Much of what we believe about ourselves isn't actually ours; it's inherited. These beliefs are often absorbed quietly and unconsciously, passed down by well-meaning (or wounded) caregivers, shaped by early experiences, and reinforced by school, culture, religion, and the environments in which we grew up. We internalize messages about our worth, our roles, and our limitations long before we have the awareness to question them.

A child who was told to be "seen and not heard" may grow into an adult who believes their voice is too much, or not enough. If someone grows up in a family where emotions are ignored, they may feel ashamed for being sensitive or expressive. These unconscious assumptions or beliefs shape how we see ourselves, how we treat others, and how we see the world. Yet, we rarely pause to ask where these beliefs came from or if they are even true.

We may say "yes" out of guilt, over-function in relationships to earn love, or shrink ourselves to avoid judgment, all without realizing that these are inherited scripts, not conscious choices. These habits of thought, behavior, and identity become so familiar that they feel like truth.

Uncovering them requires a willingness to sit with discomfort, to listen inwardly, and to become curious about what we've normalized. It's not about blaming the past, but about reclaiming agency over what we carry forward. When we become aware of the beliefs that were never truly ours to begin with, we create space to choose differently. We begin to write a new story, one that is aligned not with fear or programming, but with truth, freedom, and self-compassion.

> *"We are what we repeatedly do. Excellence, then, is not an act, but a habit."*
>
> — Aristotle

Examples:

- You hide your needs because asking felt unsafe growing up. Now you're praised for being "low maintenance," but it's costing you your truth.

- You think resting is lazy. Why? Because hustle was love in your family, slowing down felt selfish.

- You wave off compliments because pride feels dangerous, maybe even punishable.

Self-reflection lets you ask:

"Whose belief is this, and do I want to keep carrying it?"

The Villain. The Black Sheep.

In my family, I became the one they pointed at when things went wrong. The one who made too much noise. Asked too many questions. I felt too deeply. Spoke too honestly. I didn't fit neatly into the box they built for me. And so, over time, I became what they feared most, the disruptor of the illusion.

The villain.

The black sheep.

At first, I fought it. I tried to explain myself. I tried to make them see the truth, that I wasn't trying to hurt anyone, I was just trying to be real. But families, especially ones built on unspoken rules and buried pain, don't always welcome truth-tellers. I wasn't following the script. I wasn't pretending things were fine. I was breaking the cycle, and that made me dangerous.

So, they called me dramatic. Too sensitive. Selfish. Ungrateful. They turned their silence into a wall I couldn't climb. And I spent years trying to prove them wrong. Trying to prove that I was good, worthy, lovable. That I wasn't the villain they made me out to be.

But here's what I've come to learn: sometimes when you stop playing the role that kept the dysfunction running smoothly, you'll be cast as the enemy. Sometimes the one who walks away from the pattern is the one who gets blamed for it.

What I didn't realize back then was that I, too, had picked up unconscious habits. I had learned to define my worth by how others saw me. I had learned to question my instincts if they made other people uncomfortable. I had internalized the belief that if people were upset with me, I must have done something wrong.

But those were *their* wounds. Their projections. And I was carrying them as if they were mine.

Mirror work helped me see this. When I looked into the mirror, not just with my eyes, but with honesty and compassion. I began to see beyond the labels. I saw the strength it took to speak up when staying silent would have been the easier option. I saw the courage it took to set boundaries, even if others called me difficult. I saw a woman who refused to abandon herself just to be accepted.

I am not the villain.

I am not the black sheep.

I am the cycle breaker.

The truth teller.

The one who chose healing over hiding.

And while it still hurts that they couldn't see me clearly, I no longer need their version of me to define who I am. I've learned to see myself through my own eyes, not the distorted lens of their fear or shame.

The mirror doesn't lie. And in it, I've finally found not a villain, but a survivor. A warrior. A woman who came home to herself.

III. Reconnecting with the Inner Child, Inner Voice, and Inner Wisdom

There's a part of you, tender, intuitive, alive, that you may have had to mute to survive. The part that once danced freely, spoke honestly, and felt things deeply. This part wasn't broken or wrong; it was simply unprotected in a world that may not have known how to hold it. To be accepted, to be safe, or to avoid pain, you learned to quiet your truth. You learned to blend in, to perform, to armor up.

But that part of you never left.

Beneath the conditioning, beneath the fear, beneath the roles you've learned to play, your inner child, inner voice, and inner wisdom are still waiting. Waiting for acknowledgement. Waiting to be heard. Waiting to be welcomed back.

Mirror work is a powerful way to reconnect with yourself. When you slow down, look into your own eyes, and listen, not just with your ears but with your heart, the gap between who you are now and who you've always been begins to close. You start feeling that quiet inner voice again, the one that speaks through feelings, longing, and gentle knowing. You begin to hear your truth, not the version of yourself shaped by the world, but the version that was whole before the world interfered.

Reconnecting with your inner child means tending to the parts of you that were hurt, silenced, or neglected. It means offering yourself the compassion, protection, and unconditional love you might have longed for back then. Reconnecting with your inner voice means honoring what you *really* feel, want, and need, instead of what you've been told you *should*. Reconnecting with your inner wisdom means trusting that there's a deeper intelligence within you. One that remembers who you are beyond fear, shame, or survival.

This reconnection is not about returning to the past; it's about integrating it. It's about becoming whole again. Each time you show up for yourself with honesty and compassion, you reclaim another piece of your power.

"Within every adult there lurks a child—an eternal child... always becoming, never completed..."

— C.G. Jung

"Be Quiet," "Sit Still,"

When I was a kid, I was a blur of energy, a wild, loud, and incredibly clumsy girl. I'd spend hours building forts in the woods, my scraped knees and torn jeans a testament to my adventures. I talked to squirrels, named the trees, and felt things so deeply that a sad song on the radio could bring me to tears.

But as I got older, the world started to ask me to be smaller. 'Be quiet,' 'Sit still,' 'Don't be so dramatic.' I learned to trade my spontaneity for approval. I traded my wildness for being 'nice.' My inner world, which once felt like a wild and vibrant forest, turned into a quiet, neatly-trimmed lawn. The girl who used to dance freely in the rain now worried about what people thought of her shoes. I grew into a strong, capable adult who could handle anything, but a part of me felt hollow.

It wasn't until a few years ago, in the midst of a personal crisis, that I realized I was living my life from the outside in. I started doing some deep work, and what I found was a little girl hiding in the corner of my soul, still scraped and messy, but also still full of life and honest emotion. She wasn't broken; she was just waiting to be seen.

37

I started small. I bought a coloring book and crayons, just for me. I began to speak up in meetings, not just with the "right" answer, but with my honest opinion. I even started to let myself cry when I needed to, without a shred of shame.

I'm still a work in progress, but now, the woman I am is built on a foundation of both the strong adult I've become and the wild, honest girl I once was. Reconnecting with her wasn't about erasing my past or pretending to be a kid again. It was about giving that part of me a voice and a loving home so that I could finally feel whole.

Real-Life Moments:

- You're terrified to start something new. That fear belongs to the child who was punished for failing.
- You can't rest without guilt. But you remember: once, you loved laying on the grass, dreaming. That part of you is still waiting for permission.
- You find clarity only when you stop trying to figure it out and instead, listen. That's your inner voice, soft and steady beneath the noise.

IV. Rewriting Old Stories & Crafting New Ones

"The most powerful stories are the ones we don't realize we're telling."

Somewhere along the way, you absorbed a story. It wasn't always told to you in words; sometimes it came in silence, in looks, in absence, or in the emotions no one dared to name. You internalized beliefs about what love should cost, who you're allowed to be, how much space you're allowed to take up, and how much joy or success you're permitted to feel before it's 'too much.'

You may carry a story that says you must earn love by fixing others. Or that your needs are a burden. Or that vulnerability equals weakness. Perhaps your story tells you that you're 'too sensitive,' 'not enough,' or that you're only valuable when you're achieving or self-sacrificing.

These stories are not your fault, but they are yours to rewrite.

Unconscious stories drive conscious choices. They shape our relationships, our self-worth, our dreams, and our boundaries. We replay them in the way we speak to ourselves, the opportunities we allow in, the love we chase or reject. And because they've lived in

38

us for so long, we often don't even question them; we just *live with them.*

But healing begins with awareness.

Rewriting your story doesn't mean denying your past. It means reclaiming the pen. It means looking at what you were taught and gently asking, *Is this still true for me?* It means grieving the lies, unlearning the patterns, and slowly writing a narrative that reflects who you actually are, not who you were told to be.

The new story might say:

- "My needs matter."
- "I can be soft and strong."
- "I am not responsible for other people's emotions."
- "I am allowed to receive love without pain or performance."
- "I don't have to shrink to belong."

You do not have to wait for permission. You are allowed to create a life that aligns with your truth, not your trauma.

Every time you speak up when you are taught to stay silent, choose to rest when you were taught to hustle, or love yourself when you were taught to hide, you are rewriting the story.

And that story? That's the one your future self has been waiting for.

"The cave you fear to enter holds the treasure you seek."

— Joseph Campbell

Flying to Escape

I used to think I was strong because I could survive anything.

I wore that like a badge of honor, the way I could push through, keep going, hold it all together while silently falling apart inside. I was the helper, the giver, the fixer, the one who smiled even when it hurt. But deep down, I was tired. Not just physically, but soul-tired from carrying emotions that were never mine to carry, from hiding pain I was never allowed to name.

It wasn't until a therapist asked me a question—simple, direct, and devastating, that something cracked.

She asked, *"Where is your little girl?"*

I didn't answer right away. My throat closed up. My heart pounded. No one had ever asked me that. Not once in all the years I spent trying to be okay.

That night, I sat in my bedroom with the lights off. I whispered into the silence, "Where are you?" I didn't expect anything. But then I felt her. Not as a ghost or a memory, but as a presence. The little girl with big eyes and a quiet ache who used to hide in corners when the yelling got loud. She had always been there, watching, waiting, hoping I'd come back for her.

She didn't need me to fix the past. She just needed me to see her.

I remembered how she used to escape by daydreaming, flying away in her mind to faraway places when home felt like a war zone. I remembered how she would sing to herself at night, just to feel less alone, how she had learned to confuse love with the delicate dance of avoiding conflict, tiptoeing around tension, believing that peace was something you earned by staying small, how she confused abandonment with her own unworthiness.

I wept for her. And then I held her in my heart, in my breath, in the way I spoke to myself.

That was the beginning.

Since then, reconnecting with her has become a practice. When I'm anxious, I ask what she's feeling. When I'm tempted to self-abandon, I ask what she needs. And when my inner critic gets loud, I remember she is listening.

That's how my inner voice was born again. Not as a judge, but as a gentle guide. One that says, *You're safe now. You don't have to prove anything. You get to rest.*

And that's where my inner wisdom grew roots from finally honoring the stories I once ignored and listening to the quiet knowing beneath my survival instincts.

This is what healing looks like for me: walking through my adult life holding the hand of the little girl I used to leave behind. Letting her voice matter. Letting her softness live. Letting her dream again, not to escape, but to finally come home.

The Healing Power of Reflection

Imagine your psyche as a well-worn suitcase stuffed with old memories, outdated beliefs, inherited patterns, and worn-out defense mechanisms. Some of these things you packed yourself in moments of pain or confusion. Others were tucked in by parents, teachers, society—often without your consent. Over time, the suitcase gets heavier, but you grow so used to carrying it, you forget it's even there.

Self-reflection is the quiet, courageous act of sitting down, opening the case, and gently unpacking its contents. You hold each item up to the light of your awareness and ask:

"Is this still mine? Does this belief, this behavior, this identity support the life I want to live or is it weighing me down?"

Some things you'll fold with care and return to the case. Others, you'll release, thanking them for what they once offered, but recognizing they no longer belong.

This work is not glamorous. It won't be captured in highlight reels or social media posts. It's slow. It's sacred. It's a return to yourself again and again, and each time with more honesty, more compassion, and more clarity.

Reflection is not about fixing yourself. It's about remembering who you were before the world told you who to be. It's about healing through awareness, through presence, and through the quiet, radical act of choosing to see yourself truly.

Lost Friendship

Losing a close friendship isn't like losing a family member, where the grief is public and the milestones are clear. It's a quieter, more ambiguous kind of pain. It's the silent deletion of years of shared history, the sudden absence of a person who knew your past better than anyone else. I've experienced this a few times in my life, and each time, it left me feeling disoriented and questioning my own worth.

One of my closest friends and I had been inseparable since high school. We were the kind of friends who finished each other's sentences, knew each other's families, and shared a collection of inside jokes that formed their own language. We stood by each other through breakups and heartbreaks. We were a constant in a world of change.

Then, slowly, subtly, things began to shift. Our conversations became shorter, our shared interests diverged, and a quiet, unaddressed tension grew between us. There was no big fight, no dramatic falling out. It was a slow fade, a gradual pulling away that left me confused and hurt. I would replay every conversation, every text message, every memory, trying to pinpoint the exact moment things went wrong. Was it something I said? Something I did? The silence was deafening, and the lack of closure was agonizing. I was so caught up in the "why" that I couldn't see anything else.

The healing didn't start until I gave myself permission to stop searching for an answer. I sat down with a journal and, instead of trying to solve the mystery of our friendship's end, I started to reflect on what it had given me. I wrote about the joy we shared, the support we gave each other, and the lessons I learned about myself through our connection. I allowed myself to grieve not just the loss of her, but the loss of that version of me, the me who was her friend.

Through this process of reflection, I realized that our friendship, while no longer active, wasn't a failure. It was a chapter. A beautiful, impactful chapter that has helped shape me into the person I am today. I stopped seeing her absence as a personal failing and began to see it as a part of my story. The sadness is still there sometimes, a gentle pang of memory, but it's no longer a gaping wound. It's a testament to the depth of what we had, and a reminder of the capacity I have to love and be loved. Reflection didn't bring my friend back, but it brought me peace, and for that, I am profoundly grateful.

Inner Mirror Work as a Path to Integration

Too often, we go through life reacting to the world around us without realizing the deeper emotional undercurrents steering our behavior. We repeat patterns in relationships, sabotage our own success, silence our voices, or stay stuck in cycles that no longer serve us. We call it bad luck, or blame others, or say, "That's just how I am." But what if these patterns aren't random? What if they are invitations to look deeper?

Deep self-reflection is about tracing these reactions back to their roots, not to blame anyone, and not to rehash old wounds unnecessarily, but to understand. Understanding brings power. Understanding brings integration. You begin to see that the version of you who shuts down in arguments is actually trying to protect a younger part of you who once felt unsafe expressing your truth. The version of you who constantly overworks might be seeking the love and approval you lacked as a child. The version of you that avoids intimacy may be protecting an unhealed attachment wound that taught you that connection wasn't safe.

This deep self-reflection helps you make peace with these parts. Instead of exiling them, you learn to integrate them. Instead of running from your pain, you sit beside it. You ask it questions. You hold space for the parts of you that were silenced, shamed, or scared. And slowly, something begins to shift, not because you've 'fixed' yourself, but because you've finally allowed yourself to be fully seen by you.

This is what this self-acceptance gives us: the power to choose again.

It is an ongoing practice. Not something you master, but something you return to. You will forget. You will resist. But every time you remember to pause, to look in the mirror of your inner life and ask, *"What's here for me to see?"* you reclaim a piece of yourself. You reclaim your life.

"You do not see the world as it is. You see the world as you are."

— Anaïs Nin

Lost and Trapped

There was a time in my life when I felt completely lost and trapped, not just by the substances I was using, but by circumstances that stripped away my sense of safety and trust. I was held captive, subjected to sexual assault, and lived in constant terror of violence threatening my very existence. Those moments were some of the darkest I have ever faced.

I didn't choose that pain, but it became part of my story. For a long time, I carried deep shame, guilt, and fear. I blamed myself, wondering if I could have done something different or if I somehow invited that suffering. But the truth is, what happened to me was not my fault. I was a survivor, not a victim.

There was also a moment when a drug dealer pulled a gun on me, a terrifying instant that shook me to my core. I remember the cold weight of the weapon, the pounding of my heart, and the helplessness that followed. That moment wasn't just about the gun; it was about the life I was living, unstable, chaotic, and full of danger.

At that time, I was homeless, hopping from one friend's couch to another, from one uncertain place to the next. No place felt like home. I was hoping, just hoping, for safety and some kind of peace. But each day brought new fears and new challenges.

Looking into the mirror now, I see not the brokenness that the trauma tried to imprint on me, but the strength it forged. I see a person who has endured unimaginable fear and pain and who is still here, still fighting, still healing.

This journey of healing is not a linear process. Some days the scars feel fresh, and the memories come unbidden. Other days, I catch a glimpse of the fierce resilience in my own eyes, a reminder that I am reclaiming my power and rewriting my story.

When I look in the mirror, I speak to myself with kindness and patience. I acknowledge my wounds and honor the courage it takes to face them. I remind myself that I am worthy of love, safety, and peace. I am learning to forgive myself and to accept all of who I am, not just the parts shaped by what I went through, but the wholeness that's always been there.

This mirror work is a sacred practice of reclaiming my identity, finding compassion for my past, and stepping into a future where my light is stronger than any shadow.

And so, every day, I choose to stand a little taller, speak a little kinder to myself, and take one more step toward the life I am creating. I am not just surviving; I am becoming whole. I am reclaiming my story, and with each breath, I remind myself: I am worthy. I am enough. I am safe.

Integration is not about becoming someone new. It's about welcoming all that you are into wholeness. Your anger, your fear, your longing, your brilliance, all of it belongs. Inner mirror work is the sacred act of becoming your own safe place. Your own guide. Your own healer.

This is how we stop repeating the past. This is how we begin to live, not from unconscious programming, but from conscious presence.

Reflection Questions for Rewriting Your Inner Story

1. What story about myself have I been carrying that no longer serves me?

_____

_____

_____

_____

_____

_____

_____

_____

_____

2. Whose voice does that story belong to, mine or someone else's?

_____

_____

_____

_____

_____

_____

_____

_____

_____

3. What version of me needed that story to survive?

_____

_____

_____

_____

_____

_____

_____

_____

4. How does this story shape my relationships, my boundaries, my goals?

_____

_____

_____

_____

_____

_____

_____

_____

_____

5. What emotions arise as I consider letting it go?

_____

_____

_____

_____

_____

_____

_____

_____

6. What truth lives underneath that old belief?

_____

_____

_____

_____

_____

_____

_____

_____

_____

_____

7. What would it feel like to forgive myself for believing it?

_____

_____

_____

_____

_____

_____

_____

_____

_____

_____

8. If I were to speak to the part of me who wrote that story,
    what would I say?

_____

_____

_____

_____

_____

_____

_____

_____

9. What new story do I feel ready to write?

_____

_____

_____

_____

_____

_____

_____

_____

_____

_____

10. How do I embody this new truth, in thought, in action, in presence?

_____

_____

_____

_____

_____

_____

_____

_____

_____

What Inner Mirror Work Offers You

- Deeper emotional awareness
- Healthier boundaries rooted in truth, not fear
- Compassion toward every version of yourself
- Life choices aligned with your soul's values
- An inner stability no storm can shake

The process of deepening self-awareness leads to profound truth. Because when you reflect deeply, you don't just look at your life. You see yourself, maybe for the first time. To reflect is also to return to Source , offering grace to the parts of you that are ready to be seen and loved.

This level of seeing requires the courage to go where the light rarely shines.

"And you? When will you begin that long journey into yourself?"

— *Rum*

Journal Prompts

1. **What is the story I tell myself about who I am?**

   Explore the beliefs you carry about your identity, your worth, your role in relationships, and your value in the world. Are these beliefs really *yours*?

   _____

   _____

   _____

   _____

   _____

   _____

   _____

   _____

   _____

2. Where did this story begin?

Trace your inner narrative back to its origin. Who helped shape it? What experiences reinforced it?

   _____

   _____

   _____

   _____

_____

_____

_____

_____

_____

_____

_____

3. What parts of my story do I feel ashamed of or try to hide?

Bring compassion to the places that feel heavy or unworthy. These parts are often trying to protect you.

_____

_____

_____

_____

_____

_____

_____

_____

_____

4. When do I feel most like the real me?

Describe situations, environments, or relationships where you feel free to be fully yourself. What do those moments say about your true essence?

_____

_____

_____

_____

_____

_____

_____

_____

_____

5. What role do I often play in my relationships (the fixer, the caregiver, the peacemaker, the rebel, etc.)?

How has this role shaped your story? What does it cost you, and what has it given you?

_____

_____

_____

_____

_____

_____

_____

_____

_____

6. Whose voice do I hear in my head when I doubt myself?

Be honest: is the inner critic really your voice or someone else's? What would happen if you stopped listening?

_____

_____

_____

_____

_____

_____

_____

_____

_____

_____

_____

7. What belief about myself am I finally ready to let go of?

This could be a belief like *"I'm too much," "I'm not enough,"* or *"I don't belong."* Write it out and then rewrite it with truth and love.

_____

_____

_____

_____

_____

_____

_____

_____

_____

_____

_____

_____

8. If I could rewrite my story from a place of healing and empowerment, how would it begin?

Use this as a creative reframe. Start with *"I am learning..."* or *"I now know..."* or *"The truth is..."*

_____

_____

_____

_____

_____

_____

_____

_____

_____

9. What has my pain taught me about my strength?

Pain is often a teacher. What wisdom has grown from your wounds?

_____

_____

_____

_____

_____

_____

_____

_____

_____

_____

_____

10. What chapter of my life is closing, and what chapter is asking to begin?

Reflect on the transitions happening inside you. What are you outgrowing, and what are you being called into?

_____

_____

_____

_____

_____

_____

_____

_____

_____

_____

Chapter 3: Meeting the Shadow with Compassion

"One does not become enlightened by imagining figures of light, but by making the darkness conscious."

— Carl G. Jung

Carl G. Jung taught that one does not become enlightened by imagining figures of light, but by making the darkness conscious. This is the next necessary step. We all carry a version of ourselves that we rarely, if ever, show the world. This is the shadow, the parts of ourselves that were pushed away, ignored, suppressed, or denied along the way.

It's not a flaw. It's not a moral failing. It's not a sign that something is wrong with you.

The shadow is simply the hidden side of you, the parts of yourself that were pushed away, ignored, suppressed, or denied along the way. It holds the feelings you weren't allowed to show, the behaviors you were punished for expressing, the thoughts you feared would make you unworthy of love.

We learn early in life what parts of us are "acceptable" and what parts are not.

So, we adapt.

We smile instead of cry.

We comply instead of questioning.

We excel instead of rest.

We armor up instead of asking for help.

And what doesn't fit into that polished, presentable self gets pushed underground, into the shadows.

But the shadow doesn't go away just because we ignore it.

It waits.

It leaks.

It comes out sideways through our triggers, our reactions, our harsh judgments of others, our inability to receive love, our self-sabotage, our rage, our anxiety, our perfectionism, and our numbing.

It shows up as the parent we swore we'd never become.

The partner who suddenly withdraws when love gets too close.

The adult who still feels like a scared child when conflict arises.

The more we deny the shadow, the more control it has over us.

The work, then, is not to banish it but to **meet it.**

To become curious instead of critical.

To turn toward our triggers, not run from them.

To see our jealousy as a compass, not a curse.

To understand our rage as grief with armor.

To recognize our shame as the echo of old wounds, not evidence of who we are.

When you begin shadow work, you are not becoming someone new; you are **remembering who you were before the world told you who to be.**

You are gathering the exiled parts of yourself and bringing them home.

Not to fix them. Not to erase them.

But to **understand them**, to hold space for their story, and to integrate them into the wholeness of your being.

This is not easy work. It asks for your honesty, your presence, and your willingness to feel deeply. But it is sacred work.

Because when we own our shadow, it no longer owns us.

- Letting yourself feel anger without shaming it.
- Admitting envy without collapsing into guilt.
- Naming fear without hiding behind control.
- Owning your desires without apologizing for them.
- Seeing the person, you judge as a mirror, not a threat.

Every emotion has intelligence. Every trigger is a teacher. Every projection is a portal.

You are not too broken. You are not too much.

You are a mosaic of stories, scars, dreams, and survival.

And the shadow is not here to shame you.

It's here to **show you** what still needs your love.

Meeting My Own Shadow

I remember the moment I truly met a part of my own shadow.

It was during an argument with someone I loved, one of those moments where logic disappears and emotion takes over. They said something that struck a nerve, and I snapped. Not just a little irritated—but *irrationally* angry. My voice shook. My chest burned. And I said things I didn't mean, all while knowing I was watching myself unravel.

Afterwards, I sat alone, ashamed. And for a moment, I wanted to blame them. But something inside whispered: *This isn't about them. This is about you.*

I journaled, traced the feeling, and found its roots not in that conversation but in childhood.

In the version of me who felt ignored. Who learned that the only way to be heard was to raise her voice.

That shadow so carefully hidden under decades of "emotional control" was just trying to say: *I matter too.*

That moment became a turning point. I didn't *excuse* my reaction, but I *understood* it. I saw the wound, not just the behavior. And in that awareness, I found compassion.

That's the invitation of shadow work.

To stop running from what you feel.

To stop pretending you've evolved past human emotion.

To be honest about the parts of you that ache, rage, fear, or fall short, and instead of punishing those parts, *bring them into the light with tenderness.*

Compassion is the key. Without it, shadow work becomes another self-improvement checklist. But with compassion, it becomes sacred integration. You begin to realize: your shadow isn't working *against* you; it's trying to protect you with outdated strategies. Strategies that once worked but no longer serve the life you're trying to create.

You don't have to become someone else to heal. You simply have to *welcome back* the parts of you that were never allowed to be whole.

Reflection Questions:

1. What emotions or behaviors do you tend to judge or suppress in yourself?

_____

_____

_____

_____

_____

_____

_____

_____

2. Can you remember when you first learned those parts weren't "acceptable"?

_____

_____

_____

_____

_____

_____

_____

_____

3. What is one compassionate thing you can say to that version of yourself now?

_____

_____

_____

_____

_____

_____

_____

_____

4. How does your shadow show up in your relationships?

_____

_____

_____

_____

_____

_____

_____

_____

_____

5. What would integration, not perfection, look like for you?

_____

_____

_____

_____

_____

_____

_____

_____

Shadow Work Journal Prompts: Meeting the Shadow

These prompts are not meant to be answered all at once. Move through them slowly, with kindness and curiosity. The goal is not to fix or judge yourself, but to *understand*.

1. What traits or emotions do I judge most harshly in others?

These often reflect aspects of your own shadow disowned qualities you were taught to hide.

_____

_____

_____

_____

_____

_____

_____

_____

_____

_____

2. When was the first time I remember feeling ashamed of who I was?

Describe the moment. What message did you internalize about yourself?

_____

_____

_____

_____

_____

_____

_____

_____

_____

3. What do I try hardest to hide from others, and why?

What do you fear people would think or do if they saw this part of you?

_____

_____

_____

_____

_____

_____

_____

_____

_____

_____

4. What parts of myself do I feel I have to suppress to be accepted?

Examples may include sensitivity, anger, desire, sadness, ambition, etc.

_____

_____

_____

_____

_____

_____

_____

_____

_____

5. When someone triggers me, what story am I telling myself?

Explore what deeper wound or belief might be activated beneath the reaction.

_____

_____

_____

_____

_____

_____

What Is the Shadow?

Shadow work is the sacred and often deeply uncomfortable process of turning toward the parts of ourselves we've spent a lifetime running from. These are the traits, emotions, and impulses we were told were 'too much,' 'too dark,' 'too messy,' or 'too unacceptable.' As children, we may have learned to repress our anger to keep the peace. We buried our sadness so we wouldn't seem weak. We wore smiles over shame. We shape ourselves to be likable, safe, palatable.

But what happens to all that truth we exile?

These parts of us don't disappear; they sink beneath the surface. They hide in the unconscious, in the body, and in our habits. The rage we suppress becomes a quick temper with our children. The envy we deny can turn into bitterness toward others' success. The fear we ignore can become controlling behavior. The guilt we never process becomes self-punishment disguised as discipline.

Shadow work is about making space for those hidden selves. Not to let them take over, but to understand them. To integrate them. To say: *You belong too.*

It's not just the obvious wounds, rage, envy, shame, and fear that live in the shadow. Sometimes what we repress is our joy. Our creativity. Our sensuality. Our brilliance. We tuck away our boldness because someone once told us we were 'too much.' We hid our voices because it wasn't safe to speak. We shrink to survive, then forget we were ever whole to begin with.

"There is no coming to consciousness without pain."

— Carl Jung

The work is not about becoming 'positive' all the time. It's not about erasing pain or perfecting yourself into worthiness. Real healing, *deep* healing, is about becoming whole. It's about learning to sit with your shadows instead of rejecting them. It's about gently asking: *What part of me needs to be seen right now? What truth have I pushed into the dark because it was too much for others or for me?*

When you do shadow work, you start to see that those "flaws" you hate in yourself are often just wounded strategies to get love, safety, or belonging. People-pleasing? Maybe it was once the only way you knew to stay connected. Perfectionism? Maybe it kept you from being criticized. Control? Maybe it helped you feel less powerless when everything else felt unstable.

These aspects don't make you broken. **They make you human.** And they hold important clues.

Shadow work isn't always glamorous. Sometimes it looks like crying alone in your car after a hard conversation. Sometimes it looks like admitting you were wrong or recognizing how you've hurt someone else. Sometimes it means forgiving yourself, for surviving the only way you knew how.

But it can also be beautiful.

It can be the moment you realize your anger is sacred and protecting something valuable. It's when you stop hiding your vulnerability and start speaking from it. It's when you look in the mirror and finally say, *"Even this version of me deserves love."*

The more we make peace with our shadow, the more we reclaim our wholeness. And from that place of radical self-acceptance, we begin to show up in the world not as a fractured identity trying to prove our worth but as an integrated soul that knows I am already enough.

"One does not become enlightened by imagining figures of light, but by making the darkness conscious."

— Carl Jung

This is the work. Sacred. Messy. Transformative.

And it begins with the bravery to face yourself, not just the parts you like, but all of you.

A Personal Moment

I remember a time when I kept attracting emotionally unavailable people into my life. On the surface, I'd blame them: *Why can't they just show up? Why don't they choose me?* But in one particularly honest moment of self-reflection, it hit me. I was emotionally unavailable to myself.

I abandoned my needs constantly to keep the peace. I performed well when I was exhausted. I confused love with earning approval. That pattern wasn't random; it was my shadow calling for attention.

That truth hit hard. I had been so focused on others not meeting my emotional needs that I hadn't even noticed how often I abandoned myself. I constantly suppressed my feelings to avoid conflict. I swallowed my truth to keep the peace. I wore a mask of strength when I was absolutely exhausted inside. I convinced myself that love had to be earned through pleasing, performing, or proving myself worthy. And in doing so, I repeatedly bypassed my authentic needs and neglected my inner emotional landscape.

That pattern wasn't random; it was my shadow calling for attention. It was the unhealed parts of me replaying an old story: that my emotional needs and feelings were too much, inconvenient, or unimportant. Without realizing it, I kept connecting with people who reflected the way I treated myself: distant, avoidant, and afraid of being vulnerable.

Looking back, I see now that each person who showed up emotionally unavailable wasn't just a mistake or a painful detour; they were the Source in disguise. God, in infinite wisdom, was reflecting back to me the parts of myself I had long abandoned. These people were not punishments; they were mirrors, sacred messengers sent to awaken me to my own emotional disconnection.

Each time I felt ignored, unseen, or unloved, it was as if God was gently whispering, *"Do you see how you do this to yourself?"* When I suppressed my needs to make others comfortable, when I confused people-pleasing with love, when I wore resilience like armor and denied my own tenderness, those were the moments I strayed furthest from the divine presence within me.

The Source kept showing up through these difficult relationships, not to break me, but to *wake me*. To bring me home to myself. To show me that real healing doesn't come from someone else finally choosing me, it comes from me choosing myself, fully and completely, in every moment.

Now I understand: God wasn't denying me love. God was guiding me back to *true* love, the kind that begins from within and overflows outward. Emotional availability wasn't something I needed to *get* from someone else; it was something I had to *become* in partnership with the divine. And in that sacred becoming, everything began to shift.

"The wound is the place where the Light enters you."

— Rumi

From our earliest memories, we begin absorbing messages about who we are and who we're allowed to be. These messages come from parents, teachers, peers, religious institutions, media, and the culture surrounding us. Much of it is unspoken, absorbed through tone, glance, reaction. We're praised when we behave in ways that align with what others value and punished or shamed when we show up in ways that challenge those norms.

A sensitive boy might be told to 'toughen up,' that crying is weak, or that emotions make him less of a man. Over time, he learns to bury his tenderness, sealing away his vulnerability in favor of stoicism or anger. A spirited, curious girl might be labeled 'too much' or 'bossy,' taught to make herself smaller to be more likable, more palatable, more acceptable. And so, she quiets her fire, swallows her voice, dims her light, and wears a smile that hides her discomfort.

This is the beginning of the **shadow self**, the parts of us we learned to suppress in order to survive or to be loved. The shadow isn't evil. It's simply what we've disowned.

These repressed aspects live in the background of our lives. We might see them in moments of unexpected rage, anxiety, jealousy, insecurity, or shame. They show up in our relationships, in our fears of being rejected or abandoned, in our compulsions to prove ourselves, over give, control, or withdraw. These parts act out not because they are broken, but because they were once left behind.

We didn't choose to create the shadow. We created it as a survival strategy. We adapted. We conformed.

For many, the shadow is built from trauma, experiences where our authenticity felt unsafe. A child who was criticized for expressing joy might learn to stay quiet. A teenager whose creativity was mocked may stop dreaming out loud. These wounds become buried layers of 'not enough,' 'too much,' 'unworthy,' or 'unlovable.' And the longer they stay hidden, the more power they hold.

Shadow work is the sacred process of remembering what we forgot, reclaiming what we rejected, and loving what we once believed was unlovable. It is the brave decision to turn toward the discomfort, to explore our hidden landscapes not with judgment, but with curiosity.

It's important to recognize that the shadow forms not because we are bad, but because we were human in a world that didn't always know how to hold our fullness. Understanding this dissolves shame. It opens a path for compassion for ourselves and others. When we see someone else react, withdraw, or lash out, we begin to wonder what shadow they are wrestling with too.

The roots of the shadow are tangled into our stories, but they are not fixed. Every time we pause, reflect, and bring light to the parts we've disowned, we soften the grip of the old narrative. We stop living from survival and begin living from truth.

The shadow asks:

"What part of me was not allowed to exist?"

"Whose approval did I sacrifice my authenticity for?"

"Who did I stop being me so I could be loved?"

These are not easy questions. But in the asking, something powerful happens. We reclaim our wholeness. We come back home.

"Every human life contains a potential. If that potential is not fulfilled, then that life was wasted."

— Carl Rogers

These repressed traits don't disappear. They live underground, influencing our behaviors, beliefs, and relationships. They form what Jung called the personal shadow, and it often speaks loudest in the places where we feel most stuck or reactive.

Signs Your Shadow Is Calling You In

"Owning our story and loving ourselves through that process is the bravest thing we will ever do."

— Brené Brown

- You overreact in situations that don't seem to warrant it
- You secretly judge others for traits you fear in yourself
- You sabotage opportunities or relationships
- You feel shame that you've never spoken aloud

- You suppress your voice or needs to be liked or feel safe
- You feel like two people: one who wants to grow, and one who always pulls back

These are not signs of failure. They are invitations, your shadow whispering: *"Please see me."* Because here's the truth: the shadow doesn't want to be punished, it wants to be held.

The Echo Beneath the Conversation

I was in the middle of a conversation with a friend when she interrupted me and started talking about herself. I smiled and nodded, but inside, something twisted. I felt small, like my words didn't matter. Later, instead of brushing it off or blaming her, I sat in silence and looked in the mirror.

I asked myself, *Why did that moment hurt so much?*

And then the wave came. I remembered all the times growing up when my mother would dismiss my feelings. If I cried, I was 'too sensitive.' If I got excited, I was 'too much.' I learned to shrink myself, to make space for others, to disappear emotionally so I wouldn't be criticized or shut down.

That friend wasn't the problem; she was the mirror. A reflection of an old wound I hadn't realized still lived in me.

So, I put my hand on my chest and said, *You are allowed to take up space. Your voice matters. Your presence is not a burden.*

It wasn't about blaming the past. It was about giving that younger version of me (my little self) what she never got: validation, gentleness, permission to exist fully.

1. Name the Pattern or Emotion

"First we form habits, then they form us. Conquer your bad habits, or they will conquer you."

— Drake

Start with curiosity, not judgment.

What emotion, thought, or reaction keeps showing up in your life?

What pattern do you feel caught in, whether it's people-pleasing, anger, fear, withdrawal, or over-control?

Name it. Gently. This is the first key to awareness.

2. Trace Its Roots

"What hurts you, blesses you. Darkness is your candle."
— *Rumi*

Ask yourself:

When did I first feel this?

What moment, memory, or message may have planted this seed?

What did I come to believe about myself because of it?

Your shadow often formed as a way to protect you.

3. Meet It with Compassion

"Talk to yourself like someone you love."
— *Brené Brown*

Visualize this part of you as a younger version of yourself.

A child who didn't know how to cope but tried.

What would you say to them now, knowing what you know?

Can you offer the words you once needed to hear?

4. Practice Non-Identification

"You are not your thoughts; you are the awareness behind them."
— *Eckhart Tolle*

You *have* patterns, but you are not your patterns.

You *feel* fear, but you are not afraid.

Remind yourself: "This is a part of me, not all of me."

Hold space for the feeling, but don't become it.

5. Integrate and Transform

"The privilege of a lifetime is to become who you truly are."
— *James Hollis*

Ask: What is this part trying to teach me?

How has it shaped who I am today, for better or worse?

Rather than rejecting it, invite it into conscious awareness.

Transformation begins when you stop fighting it and start understanding it.

6. Reframe with Truth

"I am not what happened to me; I am what I choose to become."
— *Carl G. Jung*

Shift from shame to self-leadership.

Instead of "I am broken," say, "I am healing."

Instead of "Why am I like this?" ask, "What is this trying to show me?"

You are not your past. You are the one who survived it and is now rewriting it.

Real-Life Examples of Shadow Healing

1. The People-Pleaser Who Found Her Voice

Shadow: Chronic people-pleasing rooted in fear of abandonment.

Pattern: Always saying yes, avoiding conflict, suppressing personal needs.

Healing Moment: In therapy, you traced this behavior back to childhood when you had to care for an emotionally volatile parent. You believed love was earned through compliance.

Integration: You began setting small boundaries, even if it caused discomfort. You learned to say "no" without apology. Eventually, you realized that love and acceptance could exist *with* honesty, not just compliance.

Shadow: Deep insecurity masked by competitiveness and arrogance.

Pattern: Constantly needing to be right, dismissing others' ideas, equating self-worth with achievements.

Healing Moment: After a failed relationship and feedback from friends, he examined the fear underneath: a belief that he wasn't enough unless he proved himself.

Integration: He began practicing humility, listened more, and allowed others to shine. In doing so, he didn't lose respect; he gained an authentic connection.

Shadow: Inner critic developed to avoid shame and rejection.

Pattern: Harsh judgment of others, perfectionism, and inability to be vulnerable.

Healing Moment: During a silent retreat, she confronted the loneliness beneath the judgment. She realized the voice she used on others was the same one used on herself.

Integration: She practiced self-compassion through journaling and mirror work. As she softened toward herself, her relationships became warmer and more accepting.

Shadow: Abandonment wound leading to emotional detachment.

Pattern: Pulling away when things got serious, using logic to shut down emotional conversations.

Healing Moment: He realized he was pushing away the very thing he longed for the connection. In childhood, vulnerability was unsafe, so he learned to suppress it.

Integration: With therapy, he slowly allowed himself to feel, express, and stay present during emotional moments. He began to rewrite his narrative: "I can be close and still be safe."

Shadow: Fear of worthlessness without constant doing.

Pattern: Burnout, overworking, never feeling "enough."

Healing Moment: A health scare forced her to slow down. You felt lost when not being productive. This led to a deeper inquiry: Who am I *without* achievement?

Integration: You began exploring joy and presence through creativity, nature, and mindfulness. You learned her worth wasn't in what you produced but in who you were.

Shadow: Repressed grief and unmet childhood needs.

Pattern: Quick to anger, emotionally distant, blaming his parents for everything.

Healing Moment: In shadow work, he wrote a letter to his younger self and realized the pain he had never acknowledged. Under the anger was sorrow and yearning.

Integration: He stopped demanding an apology from others and gave himself what he never got: validation, protection, and love. His relationships began to shift from resentment to understanding.

The Sacred Courage to Love What You Find

"To fall in love with yourself is the first secret to happiness."
— Robert M. Hanson

Shadow work is not about perfection. It's not about proving yourself healed, enlightened, or worthy. It is about becoming whole, reclaiming the parts of you that you once cast aside in order to survive, to be accepted, or to be safe. This is the sacred invitation: to make peace with your humanness, and to soften toward the parts of yourself that once felt too messy, too dark, too unlovable.

Every part of you, yes, even the parts you've judged harshly, has something to reveal. The rage you suppress may hold your boundaries. The jealousy you dislike might be showing you needs that haven't been met. The shame you carry could come from times when someone else made you feel unworthy because they didn't know how to love you. None of these parts exists to destroy you; they are simply asking to be understood.

This work is not light, but it is liberating. It takes sacred courage to turn inward and say, "Show me the truth." To see yourself clearly, not just the curated, socially acceptable version, but the raw, real self beneath the masks. And even more courage to say, "I love you anyway."

"What we resist, persists."

— Carl G. Jung

Carl G. Jung observed that the meeting of two personalities is like the contact of two chemical substances: if there is any reaction, both are transformed. This truth is why relationships are among the most powerful and clearest mirrors we face on the journey of self-awareness. Relationships have a way of showing us who we really are, revealing both our radiant light and our unhealed wounds. This is not about fixing yourself. This is about *remembering* yourself.

You are not too much.

You are not broken.

You are not behind.

You are becoming.

So, bring your fear. Bring your doubt. Bring your ache. Sit at the table with every part of your being. And listen with love.

Personal Story: The Mask I Wore

Growing up, I learned that being 'easy' to be around makes life smoother. I became the peacemaker, the one who smiled even when I was uncomfortable, the one who said ' yes' even when I wanted to scream 'no.' I thought love had to be earned by being agreeable, helpful, and never causing trouble.

I got so good at reading the room that I stopped reading myself.

When I was overwhelmed, I said I was fine. When I was hurt, I made jokes. When I was exhausted, I still showed up with a smile. People praised me for being 'so strong,' and I wore that like a badge even though inside, I felt invisible.

It wasn't until I had a panic attack in a grocery store parking lot that I realized something was wrong. I had pushed myself so far beyond my own boundaries that I couldn't even feel them anymore.

Therapy helped me name it: self-abandonment. That's what I was doing every time I swallowed my truth to make someone else be comfortable.

The first time I said, 'I can't make it today,' I felt sick with guilt. But also... relief. A quiet voice inside me whispered, 'Thank you.'

Each time I honored that voice, it grew stronger. I started asking myself, *What do I need? What do I want?* questions I had never thought I was allowed to ask.

Now, I'm learning that I don't have to earn my place in the world. I belong, simply because I exist. And every time I choose to show up as my whole self, messy, honest, real, I peel back another layer of the mask I wore for so long.

This isn't about becoming someone new. It's about remembering who I was before I learned to hide.

Reflection Questions: Meeting the Shadow with Compassion

1. What emotions or traits do I judge or hide in myself, and where did that judgment come from?

_____

_____

_____

_____

_____

_____

_____

_____

2. When did I last overreact, and what younger part of me was trying to feel safe?

_____

_____

_____

_____

_____

_____

_____

_____

3. What pattern keeps repeating, and what might it be protecting me from?

_____

_____

_____

_____

_____

_____

_____

_____

_____

4. Which part of me feels unseen or unheard, and how can I offer it validation?

_____

_____

_____

_____

_____

_____

_____

_____

_____

5. Whose voice do I hear when I feel shame or fear, and is it truly mine?

_____

_____

_____

_____

_____

_____

_____

_____

_____

6. Who or what triggers me most, and what does that say about my inner landscape?

_____

_____

_____

_____

_____

_____

_____

_____

_____

7. If my shadow could speak, what would it say it needs from me right now?

_____

_____

_____

_____

_____

_____

_____

_____

_____

8. What would radical self-compassion look like at this moment?

_____

_____

_____

_____

_____

_____

_____

_____

_____

9. What outdated story do I still believe about who I need to be?

_____

_____

_____

_____

_____

_____

_____

_____

10. What would it mean to love *all* of me, even the parts I was taught to reject?

_____

_____

_____

_____

_____

_____

_____

_____

_____

_____

Chapter 4:
The Mirror of Relationships

"The meeting of two personalities is like the contact of two chemical substances: if there is any reaction, both are transformed."

— Carl G. Jung

Relationships are among the most powerful and clearest mirrors we face on the journey of self-awareness. They have a way of showing us who we really are, sometimes in gentle, loving ways and sometimes in ways that shake us to the core. They show us both our *radiant light* and our *unhealed wounds*. Relationships remind us of how much love we are capable of giving and receiving. At the same time, they expose the fears passed down to us, the old stories we keep telling ourselves without realizing it, and the habits we keep repeating again and again.

When we're willing to look closely at our interactions with others, whether joyful or painful, we uncover the rich and layered truth of who we are beneath the surface.

Each encounter becomes an opportunity: not just to connect, but to *awaken*.

Whether it's a romantic partner who triggers our abandonment fears...

A parent whose approval we still unconsciously seek...

A sibling who reminds us of competition, comparison, or childhood roles...

A friend who reflects the way we overextend ourselves to be liked...

Or a coworker who brings up our need for control, validation, or boundaries...

Each relationship becomes a **sacred invitation** to explore the landscape of our inner world. The beautiful ones remind us of our capacity for love, joy, and connection. The difficult ones reveal our attachments, emotional reactivity, and the parts of us that are still seeking healing. When we are triggered by someone, it's often less about them and more about what *they're activating* within us. A past experience. A forgotten wound. A hidden belief.

Sometimes when we put someone on a pedestal or idealize them, it's not just about who they are. Often, it's because they remind us of qualities we once had, or wish we had, but have pushed aside, such as strength, confidence, beauty, and freedom. In this way, they act like a mirror. A mirror doesn't judge us, and it doesn't lie; it only reflects what is already there. The important part is what we do after seeing that reflection. Do we ignore it, deny it, or let it inspire us to grow? That choice is what shapes the direction of our lives.

To enter relationships consciously is to accept that the work of connection is also the work of *transformation.*

It's to say: *I am willing to be seen, and I am willing to see.*

Not just who you are, but who I am in your presence.

What I feel. What I fear. What I crave. What I avoid.

That doesn't mean we tolerate harm.

It means we *use awareness* as a tool.

We learn to ask when triggered:

- What part of me is being reflected here?
- Where have I felt this before?
- What am I believing about myself at this moment, and is it true?

The answers don't always come easily. Sometimes, the mirror is foggy. Sometimes it's sharp. But always, it offers the chance to deepen our relationship not only with others, but with *ourselves.*

Because every relationship, at its essence, is a classroom. Every connection has the potential to teach us something vital about how we love, how we protect, how we hide, and how we grow. The most intimate relationships are not those that avoid conflict or challenge. They are the ones where both people are willing to look into the mirror, together, and *not turn away.3*

It's no accident that relationships can bring us to tears one moment and lift us into joy the next.

They are not just emotional connections; they are energetic crucibles where our deepest fears, tenderest memories, and highest potentials meet.

They awaken what is unhealed and amplify what is beautiful.

They stir the parts of us that want to be loved, seen, protected, and chosen.

81

In other words, relationships *matter,* and that's why they often feel so intense.

Think about it:

- Why does a partner's silence sometimes feel like rejection or abandonment?
- Why can a friend's honest feedback pierce more deeply than a stranger's insult?
- Why do we sometimes act out of character, shutting down, lashing out, or clinging, when we care deeply for someone?

It's not a weakness. It's not immaturity.

It's an attachment.

It's *history.*

It's the invisible thread of our earliest relational experiences still tugging at the present.

From the very beginning of life, we start building an inner blueprint, a kind of map that teaches us what it means to feel safe, loved, and connected to others. This map is shaped by our earliest experiences.

If the love we received was unpredictable, we may become hyper-vigilant to changes in tone, silence, or body language.

If the love we knew was conditional, given only when we behaved a certain way, we might spend our lives trying to prove ourselves, working hard to earn approval or to feel "good enough."

And if closeness in our family comes with chaos, we may unconsciously seek out or even recreate that same chaos later in life, even when it hurts.

These are not just mental patterns; they are *nervous system imprints.*

Your body remembers the way it felt to be soothed or not soothed.

To be held or left alone.

To be celebrated or silenced.

And so, when you're in a relationship now, you're not just reacting to what's in front of you.

You're responding with your entire emotional history.

Your heart remembers. Your body remembers.

And unless you've done the work to bring those memories into awareness, they can quietly direct your responses without your conscious consent.

This is why relationships often feel bigger than they "should."

It's why a small disagreement can trigger a spiral.

Why you might freeze when someone says, "We need to talk."

Why the withdrawal of love feels like a threat, even if it's temporary.

But here's the powerful truth: this intensity is not a curse, it's a *clue*.

A guidepost pointing you toward the places that still long to be healed.

The parts of you that want to feel safe in love.

The inner child who wants to know that this time, connection doesn't have to hurt.

That it's possible to love and be loved without betrayal, abandonment, or performance.

When you begin to understand the intensity not as something to fear but something to *explore*, your entire relational landscape shifts. You stop seeing your triggers as failures and start seeing them as invitations. Invitations to pause, reflect, and offer compassion to the version of you who's reacting from memory, not from the moment.

That's the gift of conscious relationships, not just romantic ones, but friendships, family dynamics, even mentorships and work partnerships. They become *arenas for transformation*, where you learn not just how to connect with others, but how to reconnect with yourself.

Because the goal isn't to feel nothing, it's to feel *with awareness*.

To notice when a moment is echoing a past pain.

To tend to that pain without expecting someone else to fix it.

To hold space for both your past and your present without letting either define you.

That is how we grow.

That is how we reclaim the power that intensity once stole.

And that is how we begin to love with eyes open, hearts healed, and nervous systems grounded in truth.

The Reflective Power of Triggers

Triggers can be very painful. They often show up as sudden bursts of anger, jealousy, or hurt. In the moment, it can feel overwhelming, like something inside us has exploded. They are powerful signals; in fact, they are among the clearest mirrors to our unresolved inner dynamics.

Take Sarah, for example. She found herself enraged when her partner forgot their anniversary, not because the date itself was crucial, but because the oversight echoed a childhood experience of feeling forgotten and invisible. Once Sarah recognized this, she could bring awareness to her feelings instead of lashing out. This was the beginning of healing.

"If you don't know your wounds, you will continue to bleed."
— Iyanla Vanzant

Recognizing triggers as messengers rather than enemies changes the dynamic of relationships. Instead of blaming or defending, you begin to listen to your own inner child, your unmet needs, your silent pain.

Patterns We Play Without Knowing

How many times have you found yourself repeating the same relational story, even though you *swear* you want something different?

- Are you drawn to emotionally unavailable partners, endlessly hoping this time will be different?
- Do you find yourself giving too much, only to feel drained and resentful?
- Or perhaps you pull away, afraid of being vulnerable, even when you crave connection?

These patterns often originate in childhood, when love and safety were conditional or inconsistent. They become unconscious scripts we act out, sometimes sabotaging our own happiness.

The good news is that patterns can be changed once they are seen.

My Own Mirror Story

I can still picture myself standing in my kitchen, arguing with someone I loved. The disagreement wasn't even that big, but my heart was pounding, my throat tight, palms sweaty. I wasn't just responding to *them*... I was reacting to decades of unhealed memories.

At that moment, I didn't feel like a grown woman having a hard conversation. I was a little girl again, trying so hard to explain herself to a mother who never really listened. I was pleading for someone to understand me, afraid of being ignored or pushed aside, and already preparing for the emotional pain that might come. My adult brain knew I was safe, but my body, my nervous system, didn't.

It took years of inner mirror work for me to recognize how much my childhood had written my emotional script. Watching my parents betray each other while pretending everything was fine... feeling invisible in the chaos of yelling, punishments, silence, and pain. Love was conditional. Attention came with strings. Vulnerability felt dangerous.

So, I learned to walk on eggshells. I learned to become who others needed me to be. I confused anxiety with love, because unpredictability was my normal. And as an adult, I kept recreating those dynamics, chasing people who were emotionally unavailable, fearing abandonment even in safe spaces, and shrinking myself to avoid being "too much."

This is how attachment works. It doesn't just live in memory; it lives in muscle memory, in breathing patterns, in how we brace for pain we don't even expect. But here's the powerful part: once we *see it*, we can *change it*.

When I realized that the terror I felt during conflict wasn't about the person in front of me but about the ghosts behind me, I could meet myself with compassion. I could put my hand on my heart and whisper, *"You're not a little girl anymore. You are safe now. You can speak and still be loved."*

Healing happens in those moments not by erasing the past, but by holding the present with truth and tenderness.

How Relationships Teach Us Responsibility

One of the most liberating lessons relationships offer is the power to take responsibility, not for the other person's feelings or actions, but for our own emotional experience.

When you feel hurt or angry, pause and ask:

- Is this about the present moment, or an old wound being triggered?
- What is my role in this dynamic?
- How can I respond rather than react?

By owning our emotional landscape, we step out of victimhood and into empowerment.

"No one can make you feel inferior without your consent."
— Eleanor Roosevelt

Healthy Boundaries: The Foundation of Connection

Many people think of boundaries as harsh barriers, but in reality, they are more like bridges. Boundaries create clarity by showing others how we expect to be treated and by reminding us how we want to treat ourselves.

Setting boundaries can be challenging because it often triggers guilt or fear of rejection. Still, boundaries are essential if we want relationships that are healthy and lasting. They make it possible for us to stay present with others while also protecting our energy and sense of self.

Inner Mirror Work in Relationships: Practical Applications

When you begin using inner mirror work in relationships, you start to:

- Recognize emotional triggers as signs of unmet needs or past wounds.
- Communicate openly about what you feel and need, without blame or aggression.
- Discern projection, when someone's behavior reflects their inner world, not yours.
- Set compassionate boundaries that protect your energy and honor your values.

- Choose consciously whether to engage or disengage from patterns that no longer serve your growth.

Examples of Mirror Work in Action

- A woman notices she constantly feels jealous when her partner spends time with friends.

  Through reflection, she discovers she fears abandonment rooted in childhood insecurity. Instead of lashing out, she communicates her feelings and works on building trust.

- A man recognizes that he shuts down during conflicts because he learned to avoid confrontation to keep peace in his family.

  Mirror work helps him identify his fear and practice expressing himself calmly.

- Someone realizes their chronic people-pleasing masks a deep belief that they are only lovable if they are useful.

  They begin to practice saying "no" and honoring their own needs.

Definition of Healthy Boundaries

1. Emotional Boundaries

- I am not responsible for other people's feelings.
- I can hold space for someone without absorbing their pain.
- I honor my emotions without needing to justify them to others.
- I give myself permission to pause before reacting.

Boundary: *"I am not responsible for other people's emotions."*

Example: When a friend becomes upset because you can't meet up, instead of feeling guilty or over-explaining, you say:

> "I care about you, but I can't make it today. I need some quiet time. Let's try another day."

2. Physical Boundaries

- My body is sacred and deserves respect.
- I can say no to touch, closeness, or shared space at any time.
- I don't have to explain why I need rest, solitude, or silence.

Boundary: *"My body belongs to me."*

Example: If someone goes in for a hug and you're not comfortable, you gently stop them and say:

> "I'm not feeling up for a hug right now. A wave is good for me."

3. Time Boundaries

- My time is valuable, and I protect it from energy drains.
- I'm allowed to say no to commitments that don't serve me. I don't owe anyone immediate responses or 24/7 access to me.

Boundary: *"My time is valuable."*

Example: Your coworker keeps calling after work hours. Instead of always answering, you respond:

> "I'll get back to you tomorrow during work hours. Evenings are my time to recharge."

4. Mental Boundaries

- I do not engage in conversations that invalidate my beliefs or values.
- I protect my peace by disengaging from gossip, comparison, and criticism.
- I am not obligated to educate or fix others at the cost of my own mental wellness.

Boundary: *"I don't have to explain myself."*

Example: Someone challenges your beliefs or decisions in a judgmental way. You say:

> "This is what feels right for me, and I'm not looking to debate it."

5. Energetic/Spiritual Boundaries

- I shield my energy when I feel depleted or overwhelmed.
- I cleanse my space regularly and surround myself with peace and intention.
- I trust my intuition to guide who is allowed in my sacred space.

Boundary: *"Not everyone is meant to access my sacred space."*

Example: After a draining conversation, you choose to meditate or take a cleansing bath instead of picking up another call.

"I need to ground myself before engaging again."

6. Relational Boundaries

- I am not available for relationships that are manipulative or one-sided.
- I choose connection over codependency.
- I do not tolerate disrespect, even in the name of love or family.

Boundary: *"I choose relationships that feel safe and mutual."*

Example: If a romantic partner consistently invalidates your feelings, you say:

"I need to feel heard and respected in this relationship. If that can't happen, I'll need to create space."

7. Work and Purpose Boundaries

- I define my own version of success.

  I don't have to hustle to prove my worth.

  I take breaks without guilt because my value is not measured by output.

Boundary: *"I don't have to prove my worth through burnout."*

Example: You set clear availability with your clients or team:

"I don't check emails after 6 p.m. Let's pick this up in the morning."

8. Digital Boundaries

- I control my screen time and what content I consume.
- I mute, block, or unfollow what doesn't nourish my soul.
- I am not obligated to perform or overshare online.

Boundary: *"I protect my energy online."*

Example: If someone keeps sending emotionally draining messages via social media, you say:

"I need to take a break from our messages right now. Please respect that I may not respond quickly."

Reflection Questions: The Mirror of Relationships

1. What repetitive patterns do I notice in my relationships? What might they be trying to teach me?

_____

_____

_____

_____

_____

_____

_____

_____

_____

2. When someone triggers me, what old wound or belief am I reacting to?

_____

_____

_____

_____

_____

_____

_____

_____

_____

_____

3. What qualities in others do I admire or resent, and how might they connect to parts of myself?

_____

_____

_____

_____

_____

_____

_____

_____

_____

4. How do I respond when I feel unsafe, withdraw, angry, or people-pleasing?

_____

_____

_____

_____

_____

_____

_____

_____

_____

5. What needs do I expect others to fulfill that I'm not meeting myself?

_____

_____

_____

_____

_____

_____

_____

_____

_____

6. How clear and compassionate am I when I express boundaries?

_____

_____

_____

_____

_____

_____

_____

_____

_____

7. What messages about love and trust did I learn from my early caregivers?

_____

_____

_____

_____

_____

_____

_____

_____

8. In what ways do I perform or edit myself to be accepted?

_____

_____

_____

_____

_____

_____

_____

_____

9. How have I been a mirror for others' growth or pain?

_____

_____

_____

_____

_____

_____

_____

_____

10. What kind of relationship do I want to create, and who do I need to become for that?

_____

_____

_____

_____

_____

_____

_____

_____

Journal Prompts

1. **What patterns keep showing up in my relationships (romantic, platonic, or family)?**
   - What do these patterns reveal about my beliefs about love, trust, or self-worth?

_____

_____

_____

_____

_____

_____

_____

_____

2. **Have I ever mistaken control, people-pleasing, or caretaking for love?**
   - Where did I learn that dynamic?

_____

_____

_____

_____

_____

_____

_____

_____

3. **What kind of energy do I tend to attract in others?**
    ○ How might that energy reflect something unresolved or unacknowledged in me?

_____

_____

_____

_____

_____

_____

_____

_____

4. **What part of me feels activated (triggered, excited, scared, clingy, distant) around certain people?**
    ○ What is that part trying to protect or express?

_____

_____

_____

_____

_____

_____

_____

_____

_____

5. **When I feel abandoned, rejected, or unseen in a relationship, what do I tell myself about who I am?**
    o   Is that story true? Where did it originate?

_____

_____

_____

_____

_____

_____

_____

_____

6. **Who in my life has mirrored back to me my own emotional availability (or lack thereof)?**
    o   How did I respond to them? What does that say about how I treat myself?

_____

_____

_____

_____

_____

_____

_____

_____

7. **Have I ever stayed in a relationship to avoid being alone?**

    ○ What was I truly afraid of facing within myself?

    _____

    _____

    _____

    _____

    _____

    _____

    _____

    _____

8. **What does a healthy, safe, and reciprocal relationship feel like in my body?**

    ○ Have I experienced that? If not, what gets in the way?

    _____

    _____

    _____

    _____

    _____

    _____

    _____

    _____

    _____

    _____

9. **What unspoken agreements or assumptions exist in my closest relationships?**

   ○ Do they serve my growth and well-being?

   _____

   _____

   _____

   _____

   _____

   _____

   _____

   _____

10. **How do I show up for myself differently when I'm single vs. when I'm in a relationship?**

    ○ Which version of me feels more grounded or authentic?

   _____

   _____

   _____

   _____

   _____

   _____

   _____

   _____

   _____

A Final Thought on Love and Growth

Love is not a destination; it is a continuous process of growth, surrender, and rediscovery. Every relationship, whether it brings happiness or difficulty, offers a chance to understand who you truly are in a deeper way.

When you begin to see your relationships as reflections instead of fights to be won, you create space for healing. This healing not only transforms how you connect with others, but it also reaches inward, helping you repair and understand yourself. The deepest repair happens not in memory or future planning, but in the present moment, the only space where you hold true power and choice.

Chapter 5:
Honoring the Present Moment

"There is only one time, now. And it is the most important time because it is the only time when we have any power."

— *Leo Tolstoy*

As Leo Tolstoy reminds us: there is only one time, now. And it is the most important time because it is the only time when we have any power. Life today moves fast, buzzing phones, endless emails, and the pressure to always be "doing". In a world like this, slowing down and being fully present almost feels rebellious. To honor the present moment is to practice presence not just as a concept, but as a lived experience.

To honor the present moment is to practice presence not just as a concept, but as a lived experience. It's the breath you remember to take when your mind starts racing. It's the pause between heartbeats when you notice the sound of birds or the sun casting golden light across your floor. It's being with *what is*, without trying to control, escape, or fix it.

The present moment doesn't ask you to be perfect. It doesn't care about your to-do list, your regrets, or your worries. It only asks: *Are you here? Are you awake to what is happening inside and around you, right now?*

For those of us who have endured trauma, the present can sometimes feel unsafe. Our nervous systems have been trained to scan for threats, to anticipate pain, to armor up. But moment by moment, we can rewire that. By grounding into our senses, by breathing deeply, by gently witnessing without judgment, we reclaim the present as a place of refuge rather than danger.

The present moment is the only place where transformation is possible. It's the only space where you can choose differently, where you can respond instead of reacting, soften instead of harden, breathe instead of panic. In this space, healing isn't some far-off goal. It's already happening.

Honoring the present is not about bypassing the past or ignoring the future. It's about recognizing that your power lives *here*. That every second offers a doorway back to your Self.

So let this be your invitation. Slow down. Put your hand on your heart. Take one conscious breath.

You are alive.

You are here.

And here is enough

My Presence Wake-Up Call

Not long ago, I was sitting across from someone I love deeply, yet realizing I wasn't truly there. Their words floated past me like white noise while my mind raced ahead, planning tomorrow's tasks, rehashing a tense conversation from last week, and worrying about a deadline next month. When I caught myself, it felt like a wake-up slap.

How much of my life was I missing by living in the past or future?

How many moments of connection had slipped through my fingers because I was elsewhere?

That moment sparked something profound in me. It wasn't about being perfect or always "present." It was about remembering to come home, again and again, to this breath, this body, this heartbeat. Life unfolds only here, only now.

"You should sit in meditation for twenty minutes a day, unless you're too busy. Then you should sit for an hour."

— Zen Proverb

Being present isn't something you finally "achieve." It's more like coming back, again and again, to yourself. It's the simple, steady practice of releasing distractions and focusing on what really matters.

Presence Is Not Stillness, It's Coming Back

Many think presence means being perfectly calm or silent all the time. But real presence is messier than that. It's waking up in the middle of chaos, noticing your mind has wandered, and gently guiding it back to your body and breath.

It's like a river that always flows, sometimes wild, sometimes calm, but always moving us forward, if we allow it.

Why the Present Matters: Science and Spirit

- **Philosophy:** Martin Heidegger described our existence as "Being-in-the-world"—a deep engagement grounded fully in the present moment. "We do not dwell in space; we dwell in time." For him, presence was the doorway to authentic living.

- **Mindfulness:** Jon Kabat-Zinn, pioneer of mindfulness-based stress reduction, calls presence "paying attention in a particular way: on purpose, in the present moment, and non-judgmentally." Neuroscience supports this: regular mindfulness training rewires our brains to reduce anxiety and enhance emotional regulation.

- **Flow:** Psychologist Mihaly Csikszentmihalyi discovered "flow," those moments when we lose ourselves in an activity, time disappears, and pure joy emerges. These are the ultimate experiences of presence, where self-consciousness melts away, and we are fully alive.

Myths About Presence

- **Myth #1:** You need lots of free time to be present. *Truth:* Even one breath, one moment, can ground you.

- **Myth #2:** Presence means I can't have goals or plans. *Truth:* Presence enhances focus and intention; it's the foundation for meaningful action.

- **Myth #3:** I'm either present or I'm not (all or nothing). *Truth:* Presence is a practice, not perfection. It's about returning again and again.

Simple Practices to Reclaim Your Now

1. **The Three-Minute Pause**

   Next time anxiety or overwhelm takes over, pause. Breathe deeply. Feel your feet on the ground. Notice three sensations: the coolness of the air on your skin, the sound of a bird, and the rhythm of your heartbeat. This anchors you back to now.

2. **Sensory Inventory**

   At any moment, take a quick mental note: What do I see? Hear? Smell? Taste? Feel? Naming your senses pulls you out of your mind and into your body.

3. **Micro-Rituals**

   Create small acts of presence, a candle lit before journaling, savoring your first sip of coffee, pausing to say "thank you" before meals. These seemingly minor moments accumulate, transforming ordinary time into sacred time.

4. **Non-Doing Practice**

   Set aside five minutes daily to just *be*. No agenda, no phone, no distractions. Let thoughts come and go like clouds, without chasing or resisting them.

The Impact of Presence on Your Life

When you show up fully:

- **Anxiety fades.** Worry is often about what *might* happen. Being present reminds you of what *is* happening.
- **Emotions become clearer.** You see feelings without getting swept away by stories or judgments.
- **Choices feel authentic.** Instead of reacting on autopilot, you act aligned with your values.
- **Intuition whispers louder.** In stillness, your inner voice grows clearer and more trustworthy.

Personal Reflection: Presence in My Daily Life

One of the most powerful lessons presence has taught me is that *now* is enough. Not when I finish the project, get the promotion, or solve the problem, but right here, right now, with all its imperfections and uncertainties.

Some days, presence is effortless; other days, it's a battle with my restless mind. But each time I return to this practice, I feel a quiet joy, a deep connection to myself and the world around me that no distraction can replace.

Reflection Questions: Honoring the Present Moment

1. When did I last feel truly *here*, not distracted or elsewhere? What helped me get there?

   _____

   _____

   _____

   _____

   _____

   _____

   _____

   _____

   _____

2. What thoughts or worries usually pull me away from now? How can I greet them with curiosity instead of resistance?

   _____

   _____

   _____

   _____

   _____

   _____

   _____

   _____

   _____

3. What sensations am I feeling in my body right now? What might they be telling me?

_____

_____

_____

_____

_____

_____

_____

_____

4. Is there an everyday task I can turn into a small ritual to ground myself?

_____

_____

_____

_____

_____

_____

_____

_____

5. How would my life change if I trusted that *this moment* is enough?

_____

_____

_____

_____

_____

_____

_____

_____

_____

"Your task is not to seek for love, but merely to seek and find all the barriers within yourself that you have built against it."
— Rumi

Journal Prompts

1. **What emotions or sensations are present in my body right now?**
   ○ Without changing or judging them, can I simply notice them?

_____

_____

_____

_____

_____

_____

_____

_____

_____

2. **What part of today have I already rushed through or wished away?**
   - What might I have missed in those moments?

_____

_____

_____

_____

_____

_____

_____

_____

_____

3. **Where is my mind spending most of its time—past, future, or present?**
   - How does that affect my sense of peace?

_____

_____

_____

_____

_____

_____

_____

_____

_____

_____

4. **What would it look like to fully accept this moment as it is, without needing it to be different?**
   o   What resistance arises when I try to do that?

_____

_____

_____

_____

_____

_____

_____

_____

_____

5. **In what ways do I disconnect from the present moment?**
   o   (e.g., scrolling, overthinking, planning, numbing, etc.)

_____

_____

_____

_____

_____

_____

_____

_____

_____

_____

6. **What is beautiful, comforting, or miraculous about this moment right now?**

    ○   Even if it's small, can I let it be enough?

    _____

    _____

    _____

    _____

    _____

    _____

    _____

    _____

7. **What lessons does this moment hold for me, if I slow down enough to receive them?**

    _____

    _____

    _____

    _____

    _____

    _____

    _____

    _____

8. **What am I afraid will happen if I stop "doing" and just allow myself to be?**
   ○ Is that fear grounded in truth?

_____

_____

_____

_____

_____

_____

_____

_____

_____

9. **How does my breath feel right now?**
   ○ Can I take three deep, conscious breaths before continuing?

_____

_____

_____

_____

_____

_____

_____

_____

10. **What part of me longs to be seen or felt in this exact moment?**

    ○   How can I give that part some gentle attention?

    _____

    _____

    _____

    _____

    _____

    _____

    _____

    _____

    _____

    _____

A Closing Invitation

The mirror of relationships reflects your edges, your growth areas, your wounds, and gifts. The mirror of the present moment shows your essence, your breath, your heartbeat, your alive, unfolding self.

This journey of inner mirror work, shadow integration, relational healing, and presence is not a race or a checklist. It is a sacred unfolding of an intimate dance with yourself. May you walk this path with kindness and courage, knowing that what you seek is already within you, waiting to be seen, loved, and lived.

There are moments in life when we don't need more advice; we need a lifeline. Something to hold onto when the ground beneath us is shaking. For me, mantras became that lifeline.

Chapter 6:
The Healing Power of Mantras

"Words are seeds. They grow into the reality you water them with."

—Lalah Delia

As Lalah Delia observed, "Words are seeds. They grow into the reality you water them with". Mantras are sacred affirmations, concise, potent phrases imbued with intentionality and designed to focus the mind, recalibrate ingrained belief systems, and realign the self with its core truth. This "tool of the mind" is essential for sustaining the presence cultivated in the previous chapter.

We live in a world that's loud, fast, and often unkind. Everywhere we go, we hear messages telling us we're not enough, that we must achieve more, earn more, look better, and hustle harder just to feel worthy of rest, love, or peace. It's no wonder so many of us feel disconnected from our true value.

But what if healing doesn't begin with a grand breakthrough but with a single sentence whispered in the dark?

Mantras are sacred affirmations. They are concise, potent phrases imbued with intentionality and designed to focus the mind, recalibrate ingrained belief systems, and realign the self with its core truth. Far from being mere poetic echoes or spiritual slogans, mantras are living codes, vibrational instruments of remembrance, alignment, and restoration.

Rooted in ancient spiritual traditions such as Hinduism, Buddhism, Jainism, and Sikhism, the word *"mantra" comes from the Sanskrit: "manas" (mind) and "tra"* (instrument), meaning "a tool of the mind." These ancient syllables were never meant to simply soothe. They were meant to awaken, to penetrate the layers of unconscious conditioning and resonate with the soul's highest potential.

"Mantra is not just sound. It is the sound that illuminates the mind."

—Swami Sivananda

Mantras as Mirrors of Consciousness

In the context of **inner mirror work**, mantras serve as luminous reflections. They reveal what has been buried beneath layers of criticism, fear, or inherited belief and, through repetition and resonance, call those hidden truths back into wholeness. In this way, mantras operate on two levels: as both scalpel and salve, cutting through illusion while soothing the psyche.

Where shame once spoke, a mantra replaces the voice of inner punishment with sacred permission. Where the inner critic once shouted, compassion now speaks in a softer voice. And where we once felt scattered or broken, we are reminded that we were never truly broken at all, only temporarily disconnected from who we really are.

"The words you speak become the house you live in."

—Hafiz

The Neuroscience of Repetition

Mantras harness the brain's inherent neuroplasticity, the ability to rewire itself in response to repeated stimuli. Each time you recite a mantra, you're etching a new pathway across neural terrain previously carved by criticism, trauma, or fear. Mantras create cognitive dissonance in the best way possible: they challenge your limiting inner dialogue and reintroduce truth to a system trained in distortion.

This is not spiritual bypassing; it is spiritual reprogramming. Each utterance lays down a new track of identity, autonomy, and belonging.

"Affirmations are not wishful thinking. They are declarations of a future self already forming."

—Dr. Joe Dispenza

Rewiring My Trauma

For years, I didn't realize my mind had been trained by trauma. I just thought I was overly sensitive, always on edge, always bracing for something to go wrong. Growing up in a home where love felt unpredictable and affection came with conditions, I learned to stay small, quiet, and ready. My nervous system was constantly on high alert, scanning for danger even when none was there. I thought this was just who I was. But it wasn't. It was who I had become to survive.

Only when I started doing the deep work, therapy, reflection, and inner child healing did I begin to understand that my brain had been wired for protection, not connection. Slowly, with consistent care, I began to form new pathways. I stopped assuming the worst. I learned to breathe before reacting. I let myself trust, first myself, then others.

Healing didn't erase what happened, but it gave me back my power. And most importantly, it showed me that my brain wasn't broken. It was just doing its best to protect me. Now, I get to choose a new way of being.

Guidelines for Effective Mantra Practice

1. **Intentional Selection**

   Choose mantras that resonate with your current inner terrain. What part of you is most in need of reassurance, permission, or power? Let the words meet you exactly where you are.

2. **Repetition as Ritual**

   A mantra becomes medicine through repetition. Speak, write, whisper, or chant it. The power is not just in words but in your sustained engagement with them.

3. **Emotional Anchoring**

   Mantras should be felt, not just spoken. Allow the vibration of each syllable to echo through your body. Use them in moments of fear, anger, grief, or self-doubt to return to center.

4. **Sacred Integration**

   Weave your mantra into your existing practices, such as journaling, mirror work, yoga, or prayer. Infuse it into your breath. Let it be a compass you return to, not only when things are hard, but also when they are unfolding beautifully.

5. **Visible Reminders**

   Write your mantra where you will encounter it often, such as on mirrors, walls, in your journal, or on your phone. Let its presence be a visual anchor that re-centers your focus and intention.

Transformational Outcomes of Mantra Practice

- **Cognitive Realignment:** Replaces outdated inner scripts with empowered self-concepts
- **Emotional Regulation:** Provides grounding and stability in emotionally dysregulated moments
- **Compassionate Self-Talk:** Gently counters the harsh inner critic and promotes emotional repair
- **Intention Setting:** Offers clarity and direction for healing, transformation, and decision-making
- **Spiritual Embodiment:** Connects you with a higher consciousness, whether divine, ancestral, or intuitive

"The mind becomes that which it meditates upon. If you fill it with truth, it becomes true."

—Sanskrit Proverb

Personalizing Your Mantra Practice

Your mantras should be living, breathing reflections of where you are and where you're going. They are not one-size-fits-all. They are sacred declarations, evolving alongside your healing journey. Some mantras gently reach the inner child, the part of you that never felt fully seen, heard, or safe. They bring comfort, protection, and the validation you've long needed. Other mantras awaken your strongest self, the part of you that no longer fears taking up space, setting boundaries, or speaking your truth.

Some mantras are a balm to the nervous system, whispering safety into the cracks of your heart. Others are like fire, bold, electrifying, reminding you of your inner power and your right to rise. One day, your soul might crave stillness; another day, it may long to roar. Let your mantras rise to meet that need.

They are not empty words. They are keys. Keys to unlock parts of yourself that have been silenced, forgotten, or buried. When chosen with intention, mantras don't just affirm who you are; they help shape who you are becoming.

"The soul always knows what to say. The mantra simply gives it a voice."

— Anonymous

Let your voice rise. Let your soul speak. Let your healing take form, one sacred word at a time.

My Mantra, My Mirror

For me, my mantra didn't come from a book. It came from a wound.

It came from watching my parents betray each other and realizing that love was often tangled with pain, deception, and fear. It came from enduring my mother's sharp tongue and unpredictable hands. The kind of hurt that makes you question your own worth before you even know who you are.

It came from being the strong one for my siblings, when all I wanted was someone to protect *me*.

It came from being told to be quiet, to behave, to smile, and slowly forgetting the sound of my own voice.

It came from surviving… but not yet knowing how to *live*.

There was a day after yet another moment of feeling invisible, overwhelmed, and "too much" for others, where I broke down.

And in the silence after the sobs, something ancient whispered in me. Not loud. Not dramatic. Just real:

"I am allowed to take up space."

"I am not here to feel small, apologize, or disappear."

"I am the light I've been waiting for."

That became my mantra.

Not just words but a reclamation.

A remembering.

Tailoring Mantras to Your Inner Landscape

- **For Empowerment:**
  "My voice is valuable, and I use it with clarity."
- **For Healing:**
  "It is safe for me to feel and release."
- **For Belonging:**
  "I am inherently worthy of love and connection."
- **For Boundaries:**
  "Protecting my energy is an act of self-honoring."

117

- **For Forgiveness:**

  "I forgive myself for what I didn't yet know."
- **For Presence:**

  "In this breath, I return to myself."

Practical Mantra Integration

- **Morning Ritual:**

  Begin your day with candlelight, breathwork, and three mindful recitations. Set an energetic tone before the world makes its claims on you.
- **During Emotional Triggers:**

  Pause. Breathe deeply. Whisper your mantra as you place a hand on your heart or solar plexus. Let your body feel its truth.
- **Journaling Companion:**

  Start or end your journal entries with your mantra. Reflect on how it shifted your thinking or opened a new insight.
- **Mirror Practice:**

  Stand in front of your reflection. Look into your own eyes. Say your mantra slowly, as if sharing it with someone you love.

Mantras as Living Beings

A mantra is not static; it evolves with you. Some days, it may feel too bold. Other days, inadequate. This is part of the process. Resistance is not failure. It is feedback. The goal is not perfection; it is devotion. Show up again. Whisper the words again. And let them whisper back to you.

"The mantra doesn't change the world outside of you. It changes the world within you, which changes everything else."

—Nayyirah Waheed

Closing Reflections

Mantras are more than affirmations. They are invitations, doorways back to self, back to presence, back to the truth you never really lost. Their sacred repetition becomes a form of remembrance:

of who you are, of what you are made for, and of the wholeness that was never broken.

Let them live in you. Let them guide you. And when you forget, let them call you home again.

"Say the words until they say you."

—Mark Nepo

You do not need to be flawless to speak your healing into being. You need to be willing. The powerful affirmations of this practice are such as, "My words are medicine. My voice is sacred. I speak life into my journey, one breath at a time" help rewrite the internal scripts that bind you.

Yet, even with a healed voice, the ultimate test remains choosing to show that same compassion to your past self.

Day 1: What am I avoiding that keeps showing up in my life in different forms?

Example: I keep attracting unavailable partners. When I sit with it, I see that I avoid my own vulnerability, so I seek relationships that allow me to remain emotionally distant.

Daily Mantra: "I am ready to face what I've been avoiding with courage, clarity, and compassion. Each pattern is a messenger, guiding me home to myself."

_____

_____

_____

_____

_____

_____

_____

Day 2: What parts of myself do I reject or hide from others?

Example: For a long time, I hid my vulnerability. I was the one who always had it together—the fixer, the strong one, the one who never needed help. Underneath that armor was fear. Fear of being seen as weak. Fear that if I exposed the cracks, people would leave.

I also hid the part of me that still felt shame over my past. The girl who spiraled into addiction, who lied, manipulated, and hurt the people who loved her. Even in recovery, I wanted to pretend she didn't exist. I wanted to rewrite the story without her in it. But she was the one who endured the storm. She held the pain when no one else could.

Now, I'm learning to stop rejecting her. I'm learning to let people see all of me—not just the polished parts. I'm learning that honesty is a form of freedom.

Because when I hide, I disconnect.

But when I reveal, I heal.

Daily Mantra: "I give myself permission to be whole. Even the parts I've hidden or silenced are worthy of love, acceptance, and belonging."

_____

_____

_____

_____

_____

_____

_____

_____

_____

Day 3: What situations make me feel small, and where does that feeling come from?

Example: I feel small when I'm in a room with confident, outspoken people who seem to have it all together. I shrink back, afraid to speak up or share my thoughts. That feeling of inadequacy stems from childhood, when I was often told to "be quiet" or that I was "too sensitive." Over time, I internalized the belief that my voice wasn't valuable; if I spoke, I'd be dismissed or judged. I now see that this belief is outdated and rooted in someone else's discomfort, not my truth. I'm learning that I deserve space, too.

Daily Mantra: "I honor the moments that make me feel small, for they reveal where I once silenced my power. I am safe to reclaim my voice and expand into my full self."

_____

_____

_____

_____

_____

_____

_____

_____

_____

_____

_____

Day 4: When do I feel most authentic? Least authentic?

Example: I feel most authentic when I'm dancing or playing with my granddaughter. I feel the least authentic when I'm pretending to enjoy things I don't, just to keep the peace.

Daily Mantra: "My authenticity is my growth. I honor the moments when I feel aligned with my truth and gently explore the times I feel disconnected, knowing both are part of my journey."

_____

_____

_____

_____

_____

_____

_____

_____

_____

_____

_____

_____

Day 5: What do I believe I need to do to be loved?

Example: I believe I need to earn love by being useful to others. I've internalized the idea that love is conditional, something I must constantly work for rather than something I inherently deserve. I find myself overextending, people-pleasing, and putting my own needs last, thinking that if I show up perfectly, stay agreeable, and never burden anyone, I will be loved and accepted.

Mantra: "Love is not something I must earn, it's something I deserve by simply being me. I release the need to perform and embrace my worthiness as it is."

_____

_____

_____

_____

_____

_____

_____

_____

_____

_____

_____

_____

_____

_____

Day 6: Who or what triggers me, and what mirror are they holding up?

Example: My mother's judgement. I realize it reflects my own fear of being seen as incompetent.

Mantra: "Each trigger is a teacher showing me where I'm still healing. I welcome the lesson with grace."

Day 7: In what ways do I seek validation from others instead of myself?

Example: I often look to others to affirm that I'm making the "right" choices. Before I trust my own instincts, I find myself needing someone else to approve, whether it's a friend, a partner, or even a stranger on social media. I notice this especially when I share something vulnerable or creative; I anxiously await feedback to feel like what I expressed was "enough. It shows me I still crave external approval to feel worthy.

Mantra: "I validate my own worth. My truth is enough."

_____

_____

_____

_____

_____

_____

_____

_____

_____

_____

_____

_____

_____

Day 8: What does my inner critic say most often? Who does that voice sound like?

Example: My inner critic says, "You'll never be enough." It sounds like my mother and father, who constantly compared me to my siblings and others.

Mantra: "I replace judgment with compassion. I am not the voice of my past."

_____

_____

_____

_____

_____

_____

_____

_____

_____

_____

_____

_____

_____

_____

_____

_____

Day 9: What old story do I keep telling myself that needs rewriting?

Example: I keep saying, "I always mess things up and I'm not good enough." This story has held me back from taking new risks.

Mantra: "I am the author of my life. I choose a story that uplifts and empowers me."

_____

_____

_____

_____

_____

_____

_____

_____

_____

_____

_____

_____

_____

_____

Day 10: What are three values I want to live by, and how aligned am I today?

Example: I value compassion, empathy, and growth, but I realize I often suppress my truth to avoid conflict.

Mantra: "I live in alignment with what matters most to my soul."

_____

_____

_____

_____

_____

_____

_____

_____

_____

_____

_____

_____

_____

_____

_____

Day 11: When I think of safety, what comes to mind? Do I feel safe being myself?

Example: Safety looks like being able to cry without judgment. I don't always feel safe expressing my emotions.

Mantra: "I am safe to be seen, known, and loved exactly as I am.

_____

_____

_____

_____

_____

_____

_____

_____

_____

_____

_____

_____

_____

_____

Day 12: What unspoken grief am I carrying?

Example: I never grieved the end of my marriage. I acted strong but buried the sadness.

Mantra: "My voice matters. My needs are valid. I reclaim my right to express them."

_____

_____

_____

_____

_____

_____

_____

_____

_____

_____

_____

_____

_____

_____

Day 13: When did I first learn to silence my needs or feelings?

Example: I learned to silence my needs when I asked for help as a child and was told I was being needy. Since then, I've kept struggling to myself to avoid being dismissed.

Mantra: "My voice matters. My needs are valid. I reclaim my right to express them."

_____

_____

_____

_____

_____

_____

_____

_____

_____

_____

_____

_____

_____

_____

Day 14: What does my shadow want to express?

Example: My shadow screams that it feels unacknowledged and taken for granted. Underneath my calm, helpful exterior, anger, sadness, and unmet needs lie. It wants to admit that I sometimes feel jealous, insecure, or resentful, and that these feelings don't make me a bad person; they make me human.

Mantra: "I welcome all parts of myself into the light of love and awareness."

_____

_____

_____

_____

_____

_____

_____

_____

_____

_____

_____

_____

_____

_____

Day 15: What does forgiveness mean to me and whom do I need to forgive?

Example: For so long, I believed that to forgive my mother would mean betraying myself. That would somehow excuse what she did: the screaming, the manipulation, the way she made me feel small, unworthy, and unsafe in the one place that should have held me gently. But I'm beginning to understand that forgiveness isn't about absolving her. It's about loosening the grip her actions still have on my nervous system, my choices, my voice. It's about choosing to let no longer the pain she caused dictate the way I see myself or move through the world.

Mantra: "Forgiveness frees me. I let go, not to forget, but to move forward in peace."

_____

_____

_____

_____

_____

_____

_____

_____

_____

_____

_____

Day 16: What would my younger self want me to know or remember?

Example: My younger self would want me to remember how much I loved to sing, fly, and explore. I've traded that freedom for growth.

Mantra: "I carry the wisdom and wonder of my younger self with tenderness and pride."

_____

_____

_____

_____

_____

_____

_____

_____

_____

_____

_____

_____

_____

Day 17: When do I feel the need to control, and what's underneath that?

Example: I feel the need to control when plans change unexpectedly or when people don't follow through. Underneath that is fear of being disappointed, abandoned, or made to feel invisible, like I did as a child when no one showed up for me. Control gives me the illusion of safety, but what I really crave is trust.

Mantra: "I trust the flow of life. I release control and embrace presence."

Day 18: Where in my life am I over-giving or over-performing?

Example: I over-function at work, taking on others' responsibilities. It's my way of trying to be seen as indispensable.

Mantra: "My worth is not measured by my output. I am enough as I am."

Day 19: What boundary do I need to set to feel more empowered?

Example: I need to say no to family obligations that drain me. I often agree out of guilt, not desire.

Mantra: "Boundaries protect my energy and honor my truth."

_____

_____

_____

_____

_____

_____

_____

_____

_____

_____

_____

_____

_____

_____

_____

_____

Day 20: What does self-worth mean to me, and how do I honor it daily?

Example: Self-worth means not accepting crumbs in relationships. I've started to speak up more when I feel disrespected.

Mantra: "I embody self-worth by treating myself with love and respect."

_____

_____

_____

_____

_____

_____

_____

_____

_____

_____

_____

_____

_____

_____

Day 21: How do I react to rejection or abandonment?

Example: I isolate and blame myself when someone pulls away. It reminds me of feeling unwanted as a child.

Mantra: "I am never truly abandoned when I stand by myself with love."

_____

_____

_____

_____

_____

_____

_____

_____

_____

_____

_____

_____

_____

_____

Day 22: What role do I often play in relationships (e.g., rescuer, victim, fixer)?

Example: I've often been the fixer, taking on others' emotions. It makes me feel needed but leaves me empty.

Mantra: "I release roles that dim my light. I choose authenticity over performance."

Day 23: How do I want to be seen, and what stops me from showing up that way?

Example: I want to be seen as confident and creative, but I tone myself down out of fear of being judged.

Mantra: "I allow myself to be fully seen. My light is safe in the world."

_____

_____

_____

_____

_____

_____

_____

_____

_____

_____

_____

_____

_____

_____

Day 24: What emotions do I resist feeling? Why?

Example: I resist sadness. I worry that if I start crying, I won't be able to stop.

Mantra: "All of my emotions are welcome. Feeling is the first step to healing."

_____

_____

_____

_____

_____

_____

_____

_____

_____

_____

_____

_____

_____

_____

Day 25: Who do I blame for my pain, and what would taking responsibility look like?

Example: I've blamed my ex for my trust issues, but healing means I work on my boundaries and self-trust.

Mantra: "I reclaim my power by taking ownership of my healing."

_____

_____

_____

_____

_____

_____

_____

_____

_____

_____

_____

_____

_____

Day 26: When did I last listen to my intuition? What happened?

Example: I had a gut feeling not to take a new client. I turned it down and found something more aligned two weeks later.

Mantra: "My intuition is wise and trustworthy. I commit to listening deeply."

_____

_____

_____

_____

_____

_____

_____

_____

_____

_____

_____

_____

_____

_____

_____

Day 27: How have I betrayed myself to keep the peace?

Example: I agreed to help someone because I didn't want to disappoint them.

Mantra: "I no longer abandon myself. I choose peace that includes me."

_____

_____

_____

_____

_____

_____

_____

_____

_____

_____

_____

_____

_____

_____

Day 28: What is one truth I haven't spoken aloud?

Example: I feel I am not enough or too much sometimes.

Mantra: "My truth is sacred. I speak it with courage and love."

_____

_____

_____

_____

_____

_____

_____

_____

_____

_____

_____

_____

_____

_____

Day 29: What fear is holding me back right now?

Example: I fear my business will fail. My own thoughts.

Mantra: "I move through fear with faith. I am guided and supported."

_____

_____

_____

_____

_____

_____

_____

_____

_____

_____

_____

_____

_____

_____

_____

Day 30: What would my life look like if I fully embraced who I am?

Example: I'd speak confidently and surround myself with people who do not celebrate my failures.

Mantra: "I am free to be all of me. I rise in my wholeness."

Chapter 7:
The Art of Self-Forgiveness

"You cannot travel the path until you have become the path itself."
—Buddha

Introduction: The Wound Within

Every healing journey eventually reaches an important point: the confrontation with the self. Not the curated self or the socially acceptable self, but the raw, aching self-burdened by guilt, regret, shame, and unspoken grief. For many, the most difficult person to forgive is not an abuser, a betrayer, or even a parent; it is the self.

Self-forgiveness is not indulgence, denial, or bypassing. It is an act of spiritual maturity and emotional intelligence. It is the conscious decision to stop holding yourself hostage to past behaviors, choices, and unhealed parts. It is a process of returning to innocence, to wholeness, to the truth of our ever-evolving humanity.

"Forgive yourself for not knowing what you didn't know before you learned it."

—Maya Angelou

My Earliest Blueprint: A House Without Safety

I grew up watching my parents cheat on each other, one betrayal after another played out like a slow-burning soap opera in real time. There was no "safe parent," no solid ground. My mother, emotionally volatile and physically abusive, seemed more like a storm than a sanctuary. Her words cut. Her hands stung. Her moods ruled the atmosphere of every room. Some days, the silence hurt more than the yelling.

My father, though present in body, was absent in protection. He drifted behind a wall of his own denial. When he wasn't gone physically, he was gone emotionally, ignoring the chaos or, worse, justifying it. I learned early on that my pain wasn't valid, and my boundaries didn't matter.

This was my normal. And this "normal" created my identity.

How the Wound Shaped Me

I became a master of shape-shifting. I learned to read the room before I read myself. I became overly responsible, hyper-aware, and emotionally self-abandoning. I said "yes" when I meant "no." I made people comfortable at the expense of my truth. I felt safest in chaos, yet longed for peace. I didn't know how to trust.

I internalized their abuse as my fault. Their rage became my shame. Their absence became my belief that I was unworthy of love unless I earned it through pain, silence, or perfection.

This wound, the wound within, did not fade with time. It followed me into adulthood, into relationships, into the voice in my head that still sometimes says, "You're too much. You're not enough. You don't matter."

Trauma Isn't Just What Happened—It's What Didn't

Nobody ever taught me how to feel safe in my body. No one said, "You're allowed to have feelings." There were no bedtime stories, no soft shoulders to cry on, no mirror reflecting back a sense of self-worth.

The trauma wasn't just the violence. It was the absence of repair. The silence after the storm. The fact that no one ever apologized.

But here's the truth that saved me:

Healing isn't about changing the past. It's about reclaiming the present.

From Wound to Witness

There came a moment, a quiet but seismic shift, when I realized I could no longer abandon myself the way they had abandoned me. The pain of betrayal, neglect, and not being chosen had become too familiar, too comfortable. I kept looking for someone else to come save me, to make me feel worthy, to fill the ache that was never mine to carry. But no one came. And maybe that was the point.

I had to become the parent I never had. The protector I always needed. The voice that soothed instead of judging me. I had to learn how to hold myself when no one else could. It wasn't just about healing; it was about finding my way back to myself after being lost for so many years.

I began to see how I had been bleeding on people who didn't cut me, repeating old patterns in new places, expecting abandonment and rejection before it even arrived. I realized I had internalized the very harm I swore I'd escape. My survival mechanisms were noble, but they were no longer needed. What I needed now was the truth. Gentleness. Accountability. Safety.

So, I stood in front of the mirror one day, shaking but ready, and I said the words I had never heard but always needed: **"I see you. I believe you. I will never leave you."**

That moment didn't erase the wounds, but it began to transform them. I was no longer just the one who had been hurt. I was now the one who could hold the hurt with compassion. I had become the witness. The guardian. The healer.

And in that shift, from wound to witness, I reclaimed my power.

Healing the wound within has been a slow, sacred, nonlinear process. It has required me to:

- Mourning the childhood I never had
- Set boundaries with people I once bent over backwards to please
- Feel emotions I had locked away for decades
- Speak the truth, even when my voice trembled
- Let go of the fantasy that they would become who I needed them to be

The Psychological Weight of Guilt and Shame

Guilt and shame are often confused, yet they operate differently in the psyche. Guilt says, *"I did something bad."* Shame whispers, *"I am bad."* While guilt can be a catalyst for growth and restitution, shame is a psychic toxin that fractures the self.

Unchecked shame distorts our inner mirror. It creates internal narratives like "I'm unworthy of love," "I ruin everything," or "I can never be whole." These beliefs, when reinforced over time, lead to self-sabotage, emotional isolation, and blocked intimacy.

"Shame corrodes the very part of us that believes we are capable of change."
—Brené Brown

True self-forgiveness doesn't mean absolving responsibility; it means metabolizing guilt into wisdom and transforming shame into self-compassion.

Guilt says, "I did something bad." Shame whispers, "I am bad."

The moment I knew things would never be the same wasn't loud. It wasn't a slammed door or a screaming match. It was quite devastatingly quiet.

My son had stopped looking at me the same way. There was a distance in his eyes, a shift in how he spoke to me or didn't. I can't even name the one moment that broke it. It was a slow unraveling. Missed cues. Sharp words. Promises I meant to keep but didn't. At times, I was too tired, too distracted, too buried in my own pain to show up the way he needed me to.

But there's one moment I always go back to.

It was during one of those exhausting weeks when everything felt like too much. Work was piling up, bills were overdue, and my nerves were frayed. My son had been pushing boundaries, talking back, refusing to listen, rolling his eyes at every word I said. Typical teen stuff, but on that day, it hit differently.

We were in the kitchen. He made a sarcastic comment under his breath as I reminded him (again) to take out the trash. I turned around so fast, the chair behind me scraped the floor.

I snapped.

My voice got loud. Too loud. I said things I didn't mean, sharp, cutting words that weren't about the trash at all. I saw the shift in his face immediately. His posture stiffened, his expression hardened, not with anger, but with hurt. He didn't argue back. He just said, "Forget it," and walked away.

The silence that followed was louder than the yelling had been.

At first, I told myself he needed to learn respect. But deep down, I knew what I had done. I had unloaded my pain onto him. I wasn't just parenting, I was projecting. And guilt settled in quickly.

But guilt wasn't alone.

I stood in front of the mirror and truly looked at myself. I saw the stress, the fear, the weight I had been carrying. But I also saw the truth: I was a mother doing my best with what I had in that moment.

The next morning, I knocked on his bedroom door. I sat beside him, heart pounding, and said, "I was wrong yesterday. I'm sorry for yelling. That wasn't fair to you. My reaction was about my own exhaustion, not about you or the trash." That apology was my repair, and it created a bridge between us.

But even after the bridge was built, the guilt tried to creep back in. The shame whispered, *"You're unworthy of repair"*. I realized the deepest forgiveness I needed wasn't from him, but from me.

The mirror helped me pause, reflect, and choose a different path. I chose to live with the truth: Mistakes don't make me a bad mother. Avoiding repair does.

I couldn't control if he would ever fully forgive me or stop carrying his own pain from that moment. That was his journey. My work was to accept that I could not change the past. My power lived only in the present: showing up differently now, protecting my peace, and refusing to let his perception dictate my worth.

I chose to grieve the relationship I couldn't fix and embrace the one I could: my own. I stopped carrying his feelings and started honoring mine. I keep showing up, not to prove I am perfect, but because I am present, and that is enough .

Spiritual Perspectives on Self-Forgiveness

In many spiritual traditions, the act of forgiveness is regarded as sacred, an acknowledgment of human fallibility and divine grace. Christianity speaks of grace that "covers a multitude of sins." Buddhism teaches that clinging to regret is another form of ego attachment. In the Sufi path, repentance (*tawbah*) is not humiliation, but a return to love and alignment with the Divine.

"To err is human, to forgive divine."

—Alexander Pope

These teachings remind us that forgiveness is not a weakness; it surrenders to a higher truth: that we are more than our worst decisions, more than our past selves, and always capable of renewal.

Why Is Self-Forgiveness So Difficult?

Many resist self-forgiveness because they confuse it with denial or narcissism. Others fear that if they forgive themselves, they will no longer be accountable. But true forgiveness and accountability are not opposites; they are companions.

Forgiveness says: *"I accept that I have caused harm, and I choose to evolve."* It refuses to let the pain define your future. In this way, self-forgiveness is a reclamation of agency. It is not forgetting, it is remembering differently.

"Holding onto guilt is like punishing yourself for the same crime every day."

—Unknown

Why Is Self-Forgiveness So Hard for Me?

Because the guilt runs deep. I carry the weight of not being the mother I wanted to be, not showing up the way my child needed, not being fully present, not being well. I remember the times I wasn't there, and those memories still haunt me. The silence. The missed milestones. The pain I may have caused. It's not just regret, it's grief.

Substance abuse took parts of me I didn't even know I was allowed to protect. I used it because I was in pain, but I hurt people while I was trying to numb my own. I made choices I can't undo. And while I've worked to get better, there's a part of me that still believes I don't deserve full forgiveness, especially from myself.

What makes self-forgiveness so challenging is that I know the truth about who I was in those moments, and I also know the truth about who I wanted to be. The gap between those two realities is filled with shame, and shame is a heavy thing to carry. It convinces me that healing is for other people, not for someone like me.

However, the truth is that healing doesn't mean forgetting. And forgiveness doesn't mean excuses. It means holding yourself accountable while also holding yourself with compassion. It means recognizing that the person I was then was doing the best they could with the pain, trauma, and tools they had. It means giving that version of me a seat at the table, but not the power to define who I am today.

I am healing. I am showing up. I am learning to love myself, not because I was perfect, but because I kept going when it would have been easier to give up.

Self-forgiveness is hard because it asks me to see my whole self, not just the pain I caused, but the healing I've done. And that takes courage.

The Inner Voice That Doesn't Let Up

When you grow up with a parent who holds back love, who uses your mistakes against you, or who only notices your performance and not your presence, you begin to carry a harsh inner voice. A voice that says:

"You should have known better."

- *"You don't deserve peace yet."*
- *"If you were really a good person, you'd still be paying for what you did."*

That voice may sound like your mother. Your father. A teacher. A pastor. But most painfully, it starts sounding like *you*.

Forgiveness Is Not Forgetting

There's a part of me that still believes: ***If I forgive myself, I'll forget what happened.*** I worry I'll get too comfortable, let my guard down, and become careless. So instead, I clutch my guilt like armor.

But guilt is not a guide. It's a weight.

Self-forgiveness doesn't mean we erase our past. It means we let the past ***teach*** us, not ***define*** us.

The Inner Child and the Need for Compassion

Often, the self we are most angry with is not the adult who made a poor choice, but the inner child who absorbed blame, fear, and inadequacy long ago. Until we meet that younger version of ourselves with tenderness, we continue the pattern of internal rejection.

"The curious paradox is that when I accept myself just as I am, then I can change."

—Carl Rogers

Self-forgiveness means turning toward that inner child and saying: *"You did the best you could with what you knew. I will not abandon you anymore."* This inner re-parenting is not sentimental; it is transformational.

I See You

Not long ago, I was suddenly hit by a wave of sadness. It felt old, like it came from a part of me I hadn't touched in years. I was alone in my apartment, sitting quietly, when a memory surfaced: a small

185

girl, maybe seven or eight, sitting on the edge of her bed, clutching a worn-out stuffed animal, tears streaming silently down her face.

I remembered the loneliness she felt, the ache of not being seen or heard. The quiet fear that if she showed too much of herself, she would be rejected or worse, punished. That little girl had learned to hide, to toughen up, to survive by shrinking.

And there I was, decades later, still carrying her pain in my chest.

The truth hit me like a soft but fierce revelation: that little girl needed compassion. Not from anyone else. From me.

I closed my eyes and whispered to her, *"I see you. I'm sorry you felt so alone. You don't have to be afraid anymore."*

At that moment, I realized how often we dismiss our inner child's needs. We push down the pain, bury the memories, tell ourselves we're "over it" or that "it's in the past." But those parts of us, the vulnerable, scared, longing parts, still live inside. They are waiting for our kindness.

Compassion isn't just a warm feeling. It's a radical act of reclaiming and healing. It means letting ourselves be tender with our own wounds, instead of judging or dismissing them. It means holding space for that inner child to be heard, held, and loved.

That day, I promised to care for her, to listen more closely, and to be patient with the parts of me that were still in pain. Healing isn't only about changing the past. It's about becoming the safe, loving presence we once needed but never had.

A Fourfold Path to Self-Forgiveness

1. **Acknowledgment** – Face the truth of what happened or what you regret. Be honest, not punitive. Honor your emotions without collapsing into them.
2. **Understanding** – Explore the circumstances, inner wounds, or unmet needs that shaped your behavior. What part of you was trying to protect, numb, or express something?
3. **Compassion** – Offer empathy to yourself. Speak to yourself as you would to someone you deeply love. What would you say to your younger self at that moment?

4. **Integration** – Decide how you will carry the lesson forward. This may involve making amends, setting new intentions, or simply living with greater awareness.

"Forgiveness is not about letting the other person off the hook; it's about taking the knife out of your own heart."

—Andrea Gibson

Practices for Cultivating Self-Forgiveness

- **Mirror Affirmations**

  Stand before a mirror and say: *"I forgive myself. I honor my pain. I choose to grow."* At first, this may feel false or uncomfortable. That is okay. Say it until your nervous system softens.

- **Write an Apology to Yourself**

  Address the younger or wounded part of yourself. Acknowledge what they have carried. Apologize. Affirm your commitment to never abandoning them again.

- **Ho'oponopono Prayer**

  A traditional Hawaiian healing practice:

  "I am sorry. Please forgive me. Thank you. I love you."

  Repeat it daily, even if you do not yet believe the words.

- **Embodied Forgiveness**

  Place your hands over your heart or womb space. Breathe deeply. Visualize a warm light filling your body with acceptance. Let it touch every memory, every part, every wound.

Self-Forgiveness Reflection Questions

Facing the Past with Honesty

1. What am I still holding against myself, consciously or unconsciously?

   _____

   _____

   _____

   _____

   _____

   _____

   _____

   _____

2. What mistake or moment do I replay in my mind that keeps me stuck?

   _____

   _____

   _____

   _____

   _____

   _____

   _____

   _____

3. What would I say to someone I loved if they had done what I did?

_____

_____

_____

_____

_____

_____

_____

_____

_____

Understanding the Why

4. What need, fear, or wound was I responding to when I made that choice?

_____

_____

_____

_____

_____

_____

_____

_____

_____

5. Was I doing the best I could with what I knew at the time?

_____

_____

_____

_____

_____

_____

_____

_____

_____

6. What was I trying to protect or avoid by acting the way I did?

_____

_____

_____

_____

_____

_____

_____

_____

_____

Softening the Judgment

7. What would self-compassion sound like in this situation?

_____

_____

_____

_____

_____

_____

_____

_____

_____

8. Am I expecting myself to be perfect in ways I would never expect of others?

_____

_____

_____

_____

_____

_____

_____

_____

_____

9. What part of me is asking to be heard, held, or healed, not punished?

_____

_____

_____

_____

_____

_____

_____

_____

_____

Letting Go and Moving Forward

10. What lesson have I learned from this that I wouldn't have learned otherwise?

_____

_____

_____

_____

_____

_____

_____

_____

_____

Journal Prompts

1. What am I still holding against myself and why?

_____

_____

_____

_____

_____

_____

_____

_____

2. What would I say to a dear friend who made the same mistake I did?

_____

_____

_____

_____

_____

_____

_____

_____

3. How does shame show up in my body, voice, and relationships?

_____

_____

_____

_____

_____

_____

_____

_____

4. What inner child wound might be connected to my self-blame?

_____

_____

_____

_____

_____

_____

_____

_____

5. What wisdom have I gained from my most painful decisions?

_____

_____

_____

_____

_____

_____

_____

_____

_____

Soul-Centered Affirmations for Self-Forgiveness

1. I forgive myself for not being perfect. I was never meant to be.
2. I release the belief that I must suffer to redeem myself.
3. I am willing to see myself through the eyes of compassion.
4. My past does not define my worth or my future.
5. I can honor my mistakes without becoming them.
6. I am allowed to begin again as many times as it takes.
7. I no longer shame my younger self. I hold them with tenderness.
8. I am worthy of grace, growth, and healing.

Conclusion: Becoming the Healer You Needed

Self-forgiveness is not the final destination; it is a lifelong dance. It is the quiet, often invisible work of tending to your wounds without self-violence. It is choosing every day to treat yourself with dignity, even when you falter.

"Forgiveness is the fragrance the violet sheds on the heel that has crushed it."

—Mark Twain

To forgive yourself is to liberate your spirit from bondage. In releasing others, you release yourself. In releasing yourself, you reclaim your light. This reclamation allows us to gently turn our attention toward the most fragile and potent part of our psyche, the place where deep pain first took root.

Chapter 8:
The Sacredness of Starting Over

"Every day is a chance to begin again. Do not focus on the failures of yesterday; start today with positive thoughts and expectations."

—Catherine Pulsifer

Introduction: The Myth of Finality

We are conditioned to see beginnings as something that happens only once, at birth, graduation, marriage, or a new job. But in our inner life, beginnings come in cycles. Every day is a chance to begin again, as Catherine Pulsifer notes, urging us not to focus on yesterday's failures, but to start today with positive thoughts and expectations. Starting over is not failure; it is a sacred recalibration.

"And the day came when the risk to remain tight in a bud was more painful than the risk it took to blossom."

—Anaïs Nin

Why We Resist New Beginnings

The fear of starting over is a deeply human emotion. Whether it is ending a relationship, leaving a job, moving cities, or simply changing a belief, we often resist because we conflate familiarity with safety. The ego would rather cling to the known pain than risk the unknown possibility.

We also carry ancestral, cultural, and societal narratives about what constitutes success, commitment, and consistency. Starting over can feel like a sign of weakness or disloyalty. But growth demands reevaluation. A tree does not apologize for shedding leaves in autumn.

"You're not starting from scratch. You're starting from experience."

—Unknown

The Day I Gave Up Drugs

The day I gave up drugs wasn't a moment of fireworks or a triumphant victory. It was quiet, heavy, and deeply unsettling, a moment of brutal honesty with myself that I hadn't dared to face before.

I remember sitting alone in a room that felt both familiar and alien. The walls bore silent witness to countless nights of escapism, blurred memories, and promises I broke to myself. Around me lay the remnants of a life that had spiraled out of control, empty bottles, scattered pills, the tangled mess of my own making.

For years, drugs had been my refuge, the only way I knew to silence the noise inside. They offered a temporary peace, a numbing blanket to the relentless ache of fear, shame, and loneliness. But that peace was always fleeting, and the price grew higher with each passing day.

On that day, something shifted in me. It wasn't a grand revelation; it was more like a quiet collapse. I looked in the mirror and saw a face I barely recognized, exhausted, broken, and distant. I realized I had been running, not just from my pain, but from myself. The person I was beneath the haze had been lost for so long, I wasn't even sure if she still existed.

What I didn't realize then was how deeply we resist new beginnings, not because we don't want change, but because change means leaving something familiar behind, even if it's painful. The old ways and habits become part of our identity. They hold a strange comfort, a distorted sense of safety.

Resisting change is resisting the unknown, the uncertainty of what comes next. It's the fear that without the old coping mechanisms, we'll be exposed, vulnerable, raw, and unprotected. The resistance whispers, *"Better the devil you know than the angel you don't."*

But in that resistance, I found a mirror. The mirror reflected my own fears, my hidden doubts, and my yearning for a better life. It showed me how much I had been punishing myself and how much love I had withheld from myself.

Giving up drugs wasn't about weakness. It wasn't about shame or guilt. It was an act of courage, even though I didn't feel brave. It was the first step toward reclaiming my life, my voice, my dignity.

The road ahead was anything but smooth. The cravings hit like tidal waves. The memories I'd buried surfaced in painful flashes. Doubt and fear whispered lies. *You can't do this. You're broken beyond repair.*

But with every difficult day, I found pieces of myself that had been buried beneath layers of numbness. Moments of clarity, fleeting but real. Flickers of hope where despair once ruled.

I started to learn what it meant to live again, to be present with my emotions, to face my fears without running, to hold space for my own healing.

That day when I gave up drugs was not the end of my story. It was the fragile, beautiful beginning of a journey toward wholeness. A journey that demanded patience, compassion, and relentless faith in the possibility of change.

I'm still on that journey, and with each step I remember the moment I chose not to run away but to choose myself, the moment I came back to who I really am.

The Spiritual Invitation of the Blank Page

Each new beginning is a spiritual moment, an invitation to co-create with the Divine. The sacredness lies not in perfection, but in willingness. In humility. In presence. To start over is to consecrate your life again to what matters most: integrity, alignment, truth.

Many spiritual traditions honor the importance of renewal. In Judaism, *teshuvah* (repentance) means "return"—not just to God, but to the truth of who you are. In Hinduism, the cycle of destruction (*Shiva*) is necessary to make way for rebirth. In Christianity, the resurrection is the ultimate symbol of new beginnings.

"Behold, I make all things new."

—Revelation 21:5

Signs That It's Time to Begin Again

- You feel chronically drained or disoriented.
- Your soul feels out of sync with your surroundings.
- You're holding onto a version of yourself that no longer exists.
- You feel more fear about staying than leaving.
- Your intuition keeps whispering, *"There's more."*

When we override these signs, we delay the inevitable. The longer we resist, the louder the soul becomes, sometimes through burnout, illness, breakdown, or rupture. But even then, the opportunity to begin again remains.

"Rock bottom became the solid foundation on which I rebuilt my life."

—J.K. Rowling

Rituals of Rebirth: Honoring the Start

To sanctify a new beginning, you must witness it. Mark it. Bless it. Whether grand or subtle, beginnings deserve reverence. Consider creating a ritual to honor the threshold:

- **Write a Release Letter**

  Burn or bury it. Name what you're leaving behind.

- **Create an Altar of Intention**

  Place objects that symbolize your new values, dreams, or energy.

- **Anoint Yourself with Oil or Water**

  Symbolize purification. Say: *"I anoint myself for this next becoming."*

- **Speak Your Commitment Aloud**

  "I choose to walk in truth. I allow the old to fall away. I trust what is emerging."

From Rupture to Resurrection

Not all new beginnings feel triumphant. Some begin in ashes. A divorce. A death. A betrayal. In these moments, starting over feels less like a choice and more like survival. But even here, there is holiness.

The art is not in avoiding rupture but in how you rise from it. Grief and growth are not opposite; they are companions. Let the pain carve space for new wisdom. Let the endings teach you how to live more truthfully.

"When we are no longer able to change a situation, we are challenged to change ourselves."

—Viktor Frankl

The Sacred Recalibration: A Personal Story

I used to think starting over meant I had failed. That if I didn't finish what I began or if I walked away from something that no longer fit, I was weak, scattered, or giving up. So, I stayed too long. In relationships. In roles. In mindsets that felt familiar but hollow. I clung to the idea that God wanted me to endure when, in reality, He was calling me to evolve.

But the soul doesn't grow in a straight line. It unfolds in seasons. And just like winter gives way to spring, I began to sense a stirring inside me, a divine invitation to begin again.

For a long time, I didn't listen. I numbed it. Buried it. Silenced it with substances that promised peace but delivered only emptiness. I wasn't living, I was merely existing. Waking up in a fog, trying to make it through the day, performing the motions of life while my spirit lay dormant. I wore the mask well, but inside, I was unraveling.

Eventually, I lost everything. My health, my sense of self, and even my home. I became homeless, sleeping wherever I could, carrying shame like a second skin. I felt invisible to the world, and at times, to God. I wondered if I had already ruined everything beyond repair. There's a kind of rock bottom that strips away every illusion, and that's where I met Grace.

One day, when I looked at my reflection, I didn't see hope. I saw pain, regret, and exhaustion. And from the deepest, most broken place in me, I whispered a prayer I didn't even think God would hear:

"If You're real... Please help me. I don't want to live like this anymore."

That was my realization, not a dramatic moment, but a gentle opening inside me. Something changed. Something surrendered. It was the moment I stopped running and turned back toward the light, no matter how far I had gone.

I began to rebuild, brick by brick, day by day. I got sober. I faced the pain I used to avoid. I let God in and not the distant God I had feared, but the loving, steady Presence I had always longed for.

I went back to school, first earning my master's degree in Mental Health Counseling. Then I continued my studies and earned my PhD. It wasn't easy. I studied while healing. I cried while learning.

But I refused to give up. Each class, each paper, each hard-earned grade was a sacred declaration: *I am not who I used to be.*

Eventually, I opened my own mental health practice. I now hold space for others the way I once needed someone to hold space for me. The same woman who once had nothing, not even a place to sleep, now helps others rebuild their lives. That is redemption. That is grace in motion.

I look back now and see that every spiral brought me closer to my center and closer to my purpose. To tell the truth. To God. And I've learned that beginning again is not failure, it's faith.

It's saying, "Lord, I trust You more than I trust what I've built without You."

It's surrender that births freedom.

It's the risk of blooming, even after a long winter.

It's the holy work of turning your deepest wounds into sacred service.

Reflection Questions

1. Have you ever experienced emotional betrayal from someone you deeply loved?

_____

_____

_____

_____

_____

_____

_____

_____

_____

2. What does it feel like when someone you hoped would validate you instead minimizes or even benefiting from your pain?

_____

_____

_____

_____

_____

_____

_____

_____

3. How do you know when it's time to walk away, not from the relationship, but from the fantasy that it could ever become what you needed?

_____

_____

_____

_____

_____

_____

_____

_____

4. What would it mean to forgive someone who has no interest in being forgiven?

_____

_____

_____

_____

_____

_____

_____

_____

_____

A New Beginning: Resurrection Isn't Always Reconciliation

Sometimes, the resurrection isn't the reunion.

Sometimes, the resurrection is you rising out of the ashes of disappointment with your head held high and your boundaries intact.

I don't hate her.

I don't wish her harm.

But I also don't need to keep my heart open to a door that keeps slamming shut.

"I let go, not because I stopped loving her but because I finally started loving me."

Closing Words

Sometimes the rupture doesn't heal with reunion.

Sometimes it heals with release.

And sometimes resurrection doesn't mean resurrecting the relationship.

It means resurrecting your voice, your worth, your boundaries, and your wholeness.

I loved her. I still do.

But I love myself more now.

And that's how I knew it was time to let go

Living from a Place of Renewal

Starting over becomes a way of life when you commit to living in truth. It means:

- Letting go of identities that no longer fit.
- Trusting seasons of stillness and in-between.
- Choosing presence over performance.
- Returning, again and again, to self-compassion.

"You do not just wake up and become the butterfly. Growth is a process."

—Rupi Kaur

Affirmations for Sacred Renewal

1. I allow what no longer serves me to fall away.
2. I trust the wisdom of my becoming.
3. Every ending is a portal to a deeper truth.
4. I am not lost; I am being reborn.
5. I choose to honor this new beginning with clarity, grace, and courage.
6. My life is allowed to evolve.
7. I walk forward, not as who I was but as who I am becoming.
8. The unknown is not a threat; it is a holy invitation.

Closing: A Life of Continual Becoming

"Beginnings are usually scary, and endings are usually sad, but it's everything in between that makes it all worth living."

—Bob Marley

To live awake is to live as a beginner. To welcome every threshold, every unexpected curve, every surrendered identity not as punishment but as part of your soul's unfolding.

The sacredness of starting over lies in your willingness to keep opening, keep loving, and keep saying yes to yourself even when you're unsure, even when it's hard, especially when it's time.

You are not behind. You are being guided. And you are allowed to begin again beautifully, bravely, and without an apology. But what is the source of this guidance? It is the knowing that dwells within.

Chapter 9:
Listening to the Voice Within Intuition and Inner Guidance

Introduction: The Quiet Knowing

Rumi wisely advised, "There is a voice that doesn't use words. Listen." In today's fast and noisy world, full of pressure, expectations, and the need for approval, the quiet voice of your intuition can feel like a language you've forgotten. Yet this inner knowing, this sacred intelligence, has been with you all along. It is the voice of your soul, your deepest truth, and your most trustworthy guide.

Intuition isn't only a luxury for mystics or empaths; it is a birthright. It's the ability to tap into wisdom beyond logic and conditioning. It's the voice of your inner self, speaking before the mind can rationalize, deny, or distort the truth. Listening to intuition is not about abandoning reason; it is about reuniting intellect with inner truth.

What Is Intuition?

From a psychological perspective, intuition is the brain's ability to draw from stored information and pattern recognition to make rapid, unconscious assessments. From a spiritual standpoint, intuition is a direct line to the soul's knowing, a felt sense that transcends time, ego, and fear.

Intuition speaks in many languages:

- A subtle bodily sensation
- A sudden insight
- An inner nudge or resistance
- A persistent dream or image
- A moment of deep peace in the midst of uncertainty

Barriers to Inner Guidance

Many of us struggle to trust our intuition because of:

- **Cultural Conditioning:** We're taught to prioritize facts, logic, and authority over feeling and knowing.

- **Trauma and Self-Doubt:** Past betrayals or mistakes may make us question our inner compass.

- **People-Pleasing and External Validation:** We silence our own truth to avoid disapproval.

- **Perfectionism:** We overthink, overanalyze, and wait for certainty that may never come.

These barriers don't mean intuition is absent. They mean we've stopped listening. But intuition, like a quiet child waiting patiently, is still there, ready to speak the moment we are ready to hear.

Reconnecting with Your Inner Voice

Reclaiming intuitive connection is not about acquiring something new; it is about remembering. Below are practices to begin rebuilding your trust in the voice within:

1. Create Stillness

The inner voice is subtle. It rarely yells. Create quiet time each day, free from distractions, whether through meditation, walking in nature, or sitting in silence.

2. Listen to the Body

Your body is often the first to sense the truth. A tightening in the chest, a flutter in the stomach, a deep breath of relief, these are all intuitive messengers. Begin to ask: *"What is my body telling me?"*

3. Ask Clear Questions

Rather than spiraling in uncertainty, try asking your intuition directly:

- "What am I not seeing clearly?"
- "What feels like the truth, even if I'm afraid of it?"
- "What would I do if I truly trusted myself?"

Then wait. You may not get an answer immediately. But it will come, often quietly, often gently.

4. Journal Your Inner Voice

Free-write from the perspective of your intuition. Begin with: *"My intuition says…"* and let your pen move. Don't edit. Let it speak.

5. Remember Past Times You Knew

Recall a moment when you "just knew" something, whether it was a red flag, an opportunity, or a subtle truth. Validate those memories. You've been connected before. You can reconnect again.

Living Intuitively in a Distracted World

Have you ever reached for your phone without knowing why, only to realize twenty minutes later you're lost in someone else's life, not your own? That's the world we live in. We scroll instead of feeling. We react instead of reflecting. But beneath the chaos, your intuition is still whispering. It never left. It's that tug in your chest, that feeling in your gut when something's off, that moment of peace when something just *clicks*. Living with intuition means learning to hear that voice again, by slowing down, getting quiet, and remembering who you are underneath the noise. It's not about perfection. It's about presence. And the more you listen, the louder your inner truth becomes, even when the world keeps shouting.

Intuition doesn't always align with social expectations or logical plans. Living intuitively may mean:

- Saying no to something "good" because it's not aligned
- Ending a relationship others don't understand
- Moving in a direction that doesn't yet make sense on paper
- Waiting when pressured to act

"The intuitive mind is a sacred gift, and the rational mind is a faithful servant. We have created a society that honors the servant and has forgotten the gift."

—Albert Einstein

To live intuitively is not to live recklessly; it is to live in attunement. The more you listen, the clearer the guidance becomes. Not all at once, but step by step.

Intuition vs. Fear: Learning the Difference

One of the most shared challenges is discerning intuition from fear or trauma response. Here are some subtle differences:

Intuition	Fear
Calm, clear, steady	Anxious, urgent, reactive
Neutral or compassionate tone	Critical or shaming inner voice
Present-focused	Future-focused catastrophizing
Subtle bodily cues	Tension, racing heart, dissociation
Rooted in self-trust	Rooted in self-protection

When unsure, wait. Ask again. Sleep on it. Intuition is patient. It does not pressure or punish.

Quotes to Anchor Your Intuition Practice

"You already know the truth. The answer is inside you."
—Oprah Winfrey

"Don't let the noise of others' opinions drown out your inner voice."
—Steve Jobs

"Follow your bliss and the universe will open doors where there were only walls."
—Joseph Campbell

"She quietly expected great things to happen to her, and no doubt that's one of the reasons they did."
—Zelda Fitzgerald

Personal Story: Learning to Trust the Voice Within

There was a time in my life when I searched everywhere for answers, books, mentors, friends, even strangers. I would ask for signs, overanalyze every situation, and second-guess myself to exhaustion. It wasn't that I didn't have an inner voice; it's that I didn't trust it.

I remember one situation clearly. I was offered an opportunity that looked perfect on paper. It paid well, had status, and checked all the "should" boxes. But every time I sat still, I felt a quiet discomfort. Not panic, not fear, just a soft, persistent knowing that said, *This isn't for you.*

I pushed it down. Told myself I was being too sensitive. I even polled people I trusted, and they all said the same thing: *"You'd be crazy not to take it."* So, I did.

And almost immediately, the quiet discomfort grew louder. I found myself drained, anxious, and out of alignment. The work wasn't bad, but it wasn't *mine*. It was like wearing someone else's skin.

Eventually, I left. Not because something dramatic happened, but because I couldn't keep silencing myself. That choice to walk away from something "good enough" in order to honor what I couldn't yet explain was one of the most powerful decisions I've ever made.

Since then, I've learned to recognize my intuition not as a booming voice or a dramatic sign, but as a subtle vibration of truth within me. It speaks through my body, my breath, and my sense of peace. And the more I listen, the more it speaks.

Learning to trust my inner guidance didn't happen overnight. It's a daily relationship, a dance of listening, doubting, remembering, and returning. But over time, I've come to realize: the wisdom I was searching for out there was quietly waiting within me all along.

Reflection Questions: Listening to the Voice Within – Intuition and Inner Guidance

1. What does my inner voice sound or feel like when I'm truly listening?

   _____

   _____

   _____

   _____

   _____

   _____

   _____

   _____

2. When have I ignored my intuition, and what were the consequences?

   _____

   _____

   _____

   _____

   _____

   _____

   _____

   _____

3. When have I trusted my gut instinct, and how did it serve me?

_____

_____

_____

_____

_____

_____

_____

_____

4. What fear or belief blocks me from trusting myself fully?

_____

_____

_____

_____

_____

_____

_____

_____

_____

5. How do I tend to confuse fear, anxiety, or past trauma with intuitive truth?

_____

_____

_____

_____

_____

_____

_____

_____

_____

6. What situations or people make it hardest for me to hear my own inner guidance?

_____

_____

_____

_____

_____

_____

_____

_____

_____

_____

7. What daily practices help me reconnect with my intuition (e.g., silence, nature, prayer, breathwork)?

_____

_____

_____

_____

_____

_____

_____

_____

8. If I paused and listened inward right now, what truth is waiting to be heard?

_____

_____

_____

_____

_____

_____

_____

_____

9. What would it feel like to trust myself even if others don't understand fully?

_____

_____

_____

_____

_____

_____

_____

_____

10. If I lived guided by my inner wisdom instead of external noise, what would I do differently?

_____

_____

_____

_____

_____

_____

_____

_____

Affirmations to Awaken Inner Guidance

1. I trust my inner wisdom.
2. My body holds the truth, and I listen with care.
3. I honor the whispers of my soul.
4. I don't need proof to follow what feels right.
5. I am open to divine direction in every moment.
6. I let go of doubt and welcome clarity.
7. My intuition leads me home to myself.
8. I am guided by something greater than fear.

Journal Prompts: Rebuilding the Inner Compass

1. When have I felt an inner knowing that proved true?

_____

_____

_____

_____

_____

_____

_____

_____

2. What does intuition feel like in my body?

_____

_____

_____

_____

_____

_____

_____

_____

_____

3. What are the fears or patterns that block me from trusting myself

_____

_____

_____

_____

_____

_____

_____

_____

_____

4. Where in my life am I being asked to listen more deeply?

_____

_____

_____

_____

_____

_____

_____

_____

_____

5. What would I choose if I genuinely believed in my inner
    wisdom?

_____

_____

_____

_____

_____

_____

_____

_____

Closing: Returning to the Voice You've Always Had

Your intuition is not a stranger; it is your original voice, the one
that existed before you were told who to be. Reconnecting with it is
not about becoming someone new but about remembering someone
ancient and wise within.

Trust does not develop through perfection. It develops through
practice. The more you listen, the more you hear. The more you
hear, the more you live in alignment not just with what is expected,
but with what is true. Your inner knowing is your only true compass.

"Your inner knowing is your only true compass."

—Joy Page

Chapter 10:
Sacred Boundaries – Honoring Your Energy, Protecting Your Peace

Introduction: The Spiritual Nature of Boundaries

Brené Brown wisely stated, "Daring to set boundaries is about having the courage to love ourselves, even when we risk disappointing others". Boundaries are often misunderstood. They are not walls to keep others out, nor are they selfish declarations of disconnection. True boundaries are sacred agreements we make with ourselves and others about what we will allow, what we will honor, and what we will no longer tolerate in the name of self-respect, integrity, and wholeness.

At their core, boundaries are about spiritual alignment. They keep you connected not just to others, but also to your own needs, values, and truth. Boundaries create an invisible structure that protects your energy, allows your voice to be heard, and gives your soul a safe place to rest.

"Love yourself enough to set boundaries. Your time and energy are precious. You get to choose how you use them."

—Anna Taylor

Why Boundaries Are Essential to Inner Mirror Work

Inner mirror work involves becoming aware of what lives inside of you, and that includes recognizing where you've allowed others to cross lines that dishonor your worth. Without boundaries, shadow work becomes unsustainable. You may continue to be re-wounded, drained, or derailed by dynamics that no longer serve you.

Setting boundaries:

- Validates your emotional and energetic reality
- Helps dismantle patterns of people-pleasing or codependency
- Allows the nervous system to feel safe
- Creates space for authentic self-expression
- Signals to the subconscious: "I matter. My experience matters."

220

Boundaries are a form of mirror work in action; they reflect the value you place on yourself.

Types of Boundaries

There are many ways to think about boundaries. Below are a few categories to help clarify your needs:

1. Emotional Boundaries

Protect your right to your own feelings. Examples:

- "I am not available for emotional dumping without my consent."
- "I won't take responsibility for fixing others' feelings."

2. Time Boundaries

Protect your schedule and priorities. Examples:

- "I don't respond to work messages after 6 PM."
- "I need 24 hours' notice for last-minute requests."

3. Energetic Boundaries

Guard your presence and spiritual space. Examples:

- "I honor my need for solitude after social events."
- "I don't share sacred experiences with people who mock or diminish them."

4. Physical Boundaries

Protect your body and physical environment. Examples:

- "Please ask before hugging me."
- "I need personal space to feel safe."

5. Conversational Boundaries

Direct how and what topics you're willing to engage with. Examples:

- "I'm not comfortable discussing my past in this way."
- "Let's change the subject; this conversation doesn't feel supportive."

The Challenge of Setting Boundaries

Setting boundaries often brings discomfort, especially if you've been conditioned to prioritize harmony over truth. You may fear being:

- Perceived as difficult
- Abandoned or rejected
- Shamed for being "too sensitive"

But boundaries are not about controlling others. They are about clarity. When expressed from a place of being grounded rather than reactivity, they foster healthier relationships based on mutual respect rather than unconscious obligation.

"No is a complete sentence."
—Anne Lamott

Common Boundary Myths (and the Truth Behind Them)

Myth	Truth
"Boundaries are selfish."	Boundaries are self-respecting. They allow you to give from a place of fullness, not depletion.
"People will leave me if I set boundaries."	The right people will honor your limits. Those who don't may be attached to your lack of them.
"I have to explain or justify my boundaries."	You are allowed to set boundaries without over-explaining. Clarity is enough.

Myth	Truth
"Boundaries hurt others."	Boundaries may disappoint others, but they foster mature and honest relationships.

Steps to Build and Maintain Sacred Boundaries

1. Identify the Leak

Where in your life do you feel drained, resentful, overwhelmed, or disrespected? That's your mirror. The leak often indicates a boundary that needs to be restored.

2. Name the Need

Beneath every boundary is a core need: rest, respect, peace, space, honesty. Identify what you're trying to protect or preserve.

3. Clarify the Language

Keep your boundary clear and centered in "I" statements. For example:

- "I need to take space after arguments."
- "I'm not comfortable with that topic of conversation."

4. Expect Resistance

Some will challenge your new limits. That's okay. Let their reaction reflect their maturity, not your mistake.

5. Practice Follow-Through

A boundary with no consequences is a suggestion. Honor yourself by standing firm, even when it feels awkward.

There was a season in my life when I said "yes" to everything and everyone except myself. If someone needed something, I showed up. If there was conflict, I smoothed it over. If I was exhausted, I pushed through. I wore my availability like a badge of honor, but underneath it, I was unraveling.

The moment everything shifted wasn't dramatic; it was quiet.

One afternoon, I was driving home from yet another appointment I didn't want to be at, feeling completely drained. I

223

looked in the rearview mirror at my own tired eyes and whispered, *"I can't do this anymore."* Not because anyone else demanded too much but because I kept offering too much of myself, afraid that saying "no" would make me unlovable, selfish, or disappointing.

That night, I sat in silence and asked myself what I truly needed. The answer came like a whisper: *"Rest. Space. Honesty."*

That was the beginning of my boundary work, not with anger, but with clarity. I learned to say, "I can't today, but thank you for thinking of me." I stopped over-explaining my no's. I started checking in with my body before agreeing to anything. It felt foreign at first, awkward, even selfish. But slowly, I started feeling peace where anxiety used to live.

People didn't always understand. Some pulled away. But the right ones remained and respected the version of me that respected herself.

I learned that boundaries aren't walls to keep people out, they're doors that let the right energy in. They're acts of sacred self-respect, a way of saying, *"I love you, and I love me too."* And protecting my peace? That's not selfish, it's survival. It's healing. It's necessary.

Understanding Your Boundaries

1. What does "protecting my peace" mean to me right now? Where in my life do I feel the most emotionally or energetically drained?

_____

_____

_____

_____

_____

_____

_____

_____

2. What signs does my body or mind give me when a boundary has been crossed?

_____

_____

_____

_____

_____

_____

_____

_____

_____

Examining Patterns

4. In which relationships do I find it hardest to set or maintain boundaries? Why?

_____

_____

_____

_____

_____

_____

_____

_____

_____

5. What do I fear will happen if I say "no" or express a need?

_____

_____

_____

_____

_____

_____

_____

_____

6. Have I ever confused being available with being lovable?

_____

_____

_____

_____

_____

_____

_____

_____

_____

Communication & Self-Expression

7. How do I typically respond when someone crosses a boundary? Do I speak up, shut down, avoid, or people-please?

_____

_____

_____

_____

_____

_____

_____

_____

8. What beliefs have I inherited about saying no, resting, or prioritizing myself?

_____

_____

_____

_____

_____

_____

_____

_____

_____

9. Do I feel safe and worthy when I ask for space, time, or support?

_____

_____

_____

_____

_____

_____

_____

_____

_____

Resetting & Reclaiming

10. Where do I need to reinforce or redefine a boundary in my life today?

_____

_____

_____

_____

_____

_____

_____

_____

_____

Affirmations for Boundary Work

1. I am worthy of relationships that honor my needs and energy.
2. Saying no is a sacred act of self-love.
3. I do not abandon myself to avoid discomfort.
4. My peace is more important than others' approval.
5. It is safe to ask for what I need.
6. I honor my "yes" and respect my "no."
7. Boundaries create room for my soul to breathe.
8. My worth is not negotiable.

"Self-care is also not arguing with people who are committed to misunderstanding you."

—Ayishat A. Akanbi

Journal Prompts

1. Where in my life do I feel the most drained? What boundary might be missing?

_____

_____

_____

_____

_____

_____

_____

_____

2. What stories have I been taught about setting boundaries?

_____

_____

_____

_____

_____

_____

_____

_____

_____

_____

3. Who in my life respects my boundaries and who resists them?

_____

_____

_____

_____

_____

_____

_____

_____

4. What emotions come up when I think about enforcing a boundary?

_____

_____

_____

_____

_____

_____

_____

_____

_____

_____

5. How does my inner child respond to the idea of saying no?

_____

_____

_____

_____

_____

_____

_____

_____

_____

_____

Exercises: Embodied Boundary Practice

Mirror Dialogue

Look into a mirror and speak your boundary aloud. Watch your face, your posture, your eyes. Practice holding your ground with love and clarity.

The Boundary Map

Draw four quadrants: Emotional, Physical, Energetic, and Time. In each, list where you need to create or reinforce boundaries.

Boundary Role-Play

With a trusted friend or therapist, practice saying a boundary out loud. Notice how your body reacts. Breathe. Practice again.

Closing: Boundaries as a Return to the Self

Boundaries are not about building fortresses; they're about building foundations. They let you stay rooted while remaining open. They let you give without being emptied. They let you love without disappearing.

Boundaries are a spiritual affirmation: *"I am here. I exist. I matter."* When you protect your energy, you protect your soul's sacred space for healing, creativity, connection, and truth. Boundaries keep the poison out, but they cannot release the weight you already carry. For complete liberation, you must transmute the internal pain that remains.

Chapter 11:
The Alchemy of Forgiveness –
Transmuting Pain into Freedom

"Forgiveness is not an occasional act; it is a constant attitude."
—Martin Luther King Jr.

Introduction: Forgiveness as a Spiritual Alchemy

As Lewis B. Smedes observed, "To forgive is to set a prisoner free and discover that the prisoner was you." Forgiveness is one of the most misunderstood and underestimated aspects of the healing process. It is not about condoning harm, forgetting injustice, or minimizing trauma. Rather, forgiveness is the conscious and courageous choice to release the energetic bond that pain creates between you and the source of that pain. In inner mirror work, forgiveness is a sacred process of transformation, an alchemy that changes your relationship to the pastIn inner mirror work, forgiveness is a sacred process of transformation. Anger isn't pushed down but reshaped, grief isn't ignored but honored, and resentment slowly softens so you can reclaim your peace and strength. Forgiveness is less about excusing others and more about freeing yourself.

The Energetic Weight of Unforgiveness

When we carry old pain, our bodies store it in muscles, posture, and breath. Our minds loop stories of betrayal. Our hearts grow guarded. Unforgiveness becomes an invisible armor, protective, yes, but also heavy, constricting, and exhausting.

Symptoms of unforgiveness may include:

- Ruminating on past wounds or betrayals
- Feeling perpetually drained around certain memories or people
- Being reactive to triggers tied to a specific person or event
- Difficulty trusting yourself or others
- Chronic bitterness, sarcasm, or guardedness

The wound becomes an identity. And identity, when forged in pain, becomes a cage.

The Layers of Forgiveness

Forgiveness is not a one-time event, it is a layered, spiraling process. Each layer brings you closer to wholeness:

1. **Recognition**

   Acknowledge what happened without spiritual bypass or denial. Truth precedes healing.

2. **Emotional Validation**

   Give yourself permission to feel it all: rage, grief, disappointment. Every emotion is sacred data.

3. **Separation**

   Learn to differentiate *the action* from *your identity*. What happened *to* you is not the same as who you are.

4. **Reframing**

   Ask: What soul lesson did this pain initiate? This does not excuse the behavior but seeks meaning through it.

5. **Release**

   When ready, begin to let go, not for *them*, but for *you*. Not to forget, but to be free.

Forgiveness Does Not Mean:

- You have to reconcile with the person
- You pretend it didn't hurt
- You stay silent about the impact
- You give up your boundaries
- You excuse repeated harm

Forgiveness is not about restoring trust in *them*. It's about restoring trust in *you*, your judgment, your dignity, your voice.

Self-Forgiveness: The Inner Healing Portal

Perhaps the hardest person to forgive is the one in the mirror. We carry guilt, regret, shame, for what we did, what we didn't do, what we didn't know how to do.

"Shame corrodes the very part of us that believes we are capable of change."

—Brené Brown

To forgive yourself:

- Acknowledge that you were doing your best with the consciousness you had.
- Recognize the inner child or past version of you who was trying to survive.
- Offer compassion instead of contempt.
- Remind yourself: Healing means evolution, not perfection.

Forgiveness as Energetic Alchemy

In the language of alchemy, lead (pain, resentment) is transmuted into gold (wisdom, freedom). Forgiveness is the fire that catalyzes this transformation.

It does not erase the past; it changes your relationship to it.

It does not mean you accept injustice; it means you no longer allow that injustice to define your energy.

Quotes to Anchor the Practice of Forgiveness

"Holding onto anger is like drinking poison and expecting the other person to die."

—Unknown

"Forgiveness is the fragrance that the violet sheds on the heel that has crushed it."

—Mark Twain

"Forgiveness is not for the weak. It is for the brave who are willing to take back their power." —Yung Pueblo

"When I release resentment, I reclaim space for peace."

—Inner Mirror Teaching

There was a time I thought forgiveness meant pretending it didn't hurt. I thought it meant brushing past the betrayal, minimizing the wound, or rising above it too quickly to prove I was strong. I tried to forgive with my mind, but my heart wasn't ready. I said the words, but the pain still clung to me like smoke after fire.

It wasn't until I sat with the grief, really sat with it—that forgiveness began to feel like something different. Not a bypass.

Not a surrender to what was done. But a sacred act of reclaiming myself.

I remember the exact moment the shift happened. I was journaling one morning and wrote, without planning to: *"I'm tired of holding this pain. Not because they deserve my forgiveness, but because I deserve my peace."* That line cracked something open in me. I realized I had been drinking poison, hoping they'd feel it. But I was the one growing bitter, closed, and guarded.

Forgiveness didn't come in a grand ceremony. It came in layers. In waves. In moments of stillness when I chose not to repeat the story again. It came when I could think of them and feel sadness, not rage, when I could bless the lesson without needing to reopen the wound, when I stopped letting the pain define me and started letting it transform me.

Forgiveness became an alchemy, a turning of sorrow into wisdom, betrayal into boundaries, heartbreak into wholeness.

I used to believe forgiveness was for them. Now I understand it's for myself. It's how I relax my fists and open my heart again, not because I forget but because I choose freedom over bitterness. Because I refuse to carry what was never mine to hold.

Facing the Wound

1. Who or what am I still holding emotional weight around?

_____

_____

_____

_____

_____

_____

_____

_____

_____

2. What part of me was hurt the most in that experience—my
    trust, my innocence, my self-worth?

    _____

    _____

    _____

    _____

    _____

    _____

    _____

    _____

    _____

3. Have I allowed myself to fully feel and name the pain
    before trying to release it?

    _____

    _____

    _____

    _____

    _____

    _____

    _____

    _____

    _____

The Alchemy Begins

4. What have I learned about myself through this pain or betrayal?

_____

_____

_____

_____

_____

_____

_____

_____

5. How has carrying this resentment or grief affected my energy, relationships, or identity?

_____

_____

_____

_____

_____

_____

_____

_____

_____

6. What am I afraid will happen if I truly let go of the anger or hurt?

_____

_____

_____

_____

_____

_____

_____

_____

_____

Reframing Forgiveness

7. What does forgiveness mean to me—not intellectually, but emotionally and spiritually?

_____

_____

_____

_____

_____

_____

_____

_____

_____

8. Can I allow forgiveness to be a slow, layered process—not a destination but a path?

_____

_____

_____

_____

_____

_____

_____

_____

_____

9. Is it possible to forgive someone *without* excusing, forgetting, or inviting them back into my life?

_____

_____

_____

_____

_____

_____

_____

_____

_____

Returning to Wholeness

10. What part of me is ready to release this pain, for my own peace and freedom?

_____

_____

_____

_____

_____

_____

_____

11. What would my life feel like without this emotional burden?

_____

_____

_____

_____

_____

_____

_____

_____

12. What truth or strength in me was revealed through this experience?

_____

_____

_____

_____

_____

_____

_____

_____

_____

Forgiveness Affirmations

1. I release what no longer serves my peace.
2. I forgive myself for the choices I made in survival.
3. I am not my past; I am the wisdom born from it.
4. I choose freedom over bitterness.
5. I honor my pain, but I am not defined by it.
6. I create space for joy where resentment once lived.
7. My forgiveness is my liberation.

Journal Prompts for Forgiveness Work

1. Who or what am I still carrying emotionally, and how does it impact me?

_____

_____

_____

_____

_____

_____

_____

_____

_____

_____

2. What would it feel like to begin releasing this weight?

_____

_____

_____

_____

_____

_____

_____

_____

3. What truth have I avoided naming about this wound?

_____

_____

_____

_____

_____

_____

_____

_____

_____

_____

4. In what ways have I punished myself for past decisions?

_____

_____

_____

_____

_____

_____

_____

_____

5. What version of me needs to hear "I forgive you" the
    most?

_____

_____

_____

_____

_____

_____

_____

_____

Rituals for Releasing Pain

Fire Ceremony

Write a letter to someone you are ready to forgive or to yourself. Say everything you need to say. Burn it safely and watch the smoke rise. As the flame transforms the page, imagine it transforming your energy.

Mirror Ritual

Stand before a mirror, place your hand on your heart, and say aloud:

"I forgive you. I understand you were hurting. I released the shame. You are still worthy of love."

Cord Cutting Visualization

Close your eyes and visualize a cord of energy connecting you to the person or memory. With love, imagine cutting the cord. Watch it dissolve. Feel the space it leaves behind.

Closing: Forgiveness Is a Homecoming

Forgiveness is not about erasing pain; it's about transforming it into something sacred. It is the path to returning home to yourself, free from the ghosts of the past, open to the gifts of the present.

In releasing others, you release yourself. In releasing yourself, you reclaim your light.

Chapter 12:
Healing the Wounded Inner Child –
Restoring Innocence, Power, and
Belonging

"It is never too late to have a happy childhood."
—Tom Robbins

"The child you once were is still inside you, waiting to be seen, heard, and loved."
—Inner Mirror Teaching

Introduction: Who Is the Inner Child?

Beneath all your adult roles, duties, and masks lives the child you once were. This is the wounded inner child—a living imprint of unmet needs, suppressed feelings, and unresolved pain. As the teaching suggests, "The child you once were is still inside you, waiting to be seen, heard, and loved". To reconnect with this presence is not about becoming childish; it is about becoming whole.

How the Wounded Inner Child Shows Up in Adult Life

- People-pleasing or fearing abandonment
- Chronic self-criticism or imposter syndrome
- Emotional reactivity or difficulty regulating moods
- Fear of authority or defiance of structure
- Difficulty trusting others or trusting yourself
- Feeling unworthy of love, attention, or success

These patterns are not moral failings. They are emotional survival strategies, crafted in a time when your nervous system was still learning what "safe" felt like.

"When a child is not embraced by the village, they will burn it down to feel its warmth."
—African Proverb

My Wounded Inner Child

I was a teenager with no parental guidance.

No one to lean on, no one to show the way.

I had to walk thirteen miles to summer school, thirteen miles under the hot sun and cold winds, just to keep moving forward.

I worked two jobs, not for extra spending money or leisure, but simply so I could have clothes that weren't hand-me-downs tethered by fraying strings and food on the table.

Now, when I see the news and hear about how many missing teens are trafficked or vanishing without a trace, I wonder in disbelief how I skimmed by without falling into those dark places.

I remember being about seven years old and running away from home.

I was gone for what felt like hours.

No one came looking for me.

But if my older sister had run away, they would have sent out a rescue crew, searched every corner, and called my name until it echoed back.

I was invisible.

Unseen.

That invisibility taught me that my pain didn't matter enough to warrant a search, that my safety was an afterthought, and that love might be conditional on who I was to others, not who I was inside.

But here's what I want my wounded inner child to know now:

You survived that invisibility.

You survived the long walks and the exhaustion.

You survived the silence and the loneliness.

And though you felt unseen, you are *seen* now. You are worthy of being found, in your own time, on your own terms.

Your story matters. Your pain matters. And most importantly, you matter.

Reparenting: Giving Yourself What You Didn't Receive

Reparenting means giving your inner child the safety, care, boundaries, and validation they may have missed. You become your own safe foundation—not to erase the past, but to change how you relate to it.

What happened to me, and how did it shape me?

When I was a child, my mother's anger felt like the only language she knew. Her voice didn't just rise, it thundered, shaking the walls and the space between us. Her rage moved through our home like a storm, wild and unrelenting, leaving fear and confusion behind. She yelled. She hit. Not because we weren't lovable, but because inside her, love had become tangled with pain, and violence was the only way she knew how to express it.

I remember one day, when I was about eight years old, coming home from school. The bus pulled up to my driveway, and the moment the doors opened, I heard the laughter, sharp, cruel, and unforgiving. I looked out the window and saw my clothes, my entire wardrobe, tossed out the window, hanging from the trees like trophies of humiliation.

My mother struggled with OCD, though it was never diagnosed. Perfection wasn't just a preference; it was a demand. And if anything fell short of that impossible standard, we paid the price, sometimes physically, sometimes mentally, but always emotionally.

This was my childhood: one marked by fear, shame, and the constant tension of walking on eggshells. It shaped how I saw myself and the world, teaching me to shrink, to hide, and to survive at all costs.

This is not just my story. It is the story of so many who have felt the weight of impossible expectations and the sting of love twisted by pain.

Core Elements of Reparenting:

1. **Attunement** – Learning to tune into your needs, emotions, and bodily signals without shame or dismissal.
2. **Nurturing** – Speaking to yourself in a voice that soothes, not scolds. Giving comfort instead of criticism.
3. **Structure** – Creating routines, boundaries, and consistency that your younger self may have never known.
4. **Advocacy** – Protecting yourself when necessary. Standing up for the parts of you that were once powerless.

Reparenting: Giving Myself What I Didn't Receive

I used to chase approval as if my life depended on it, because, in many ways, it felt like it did.

Growing up, love was conditional. Praise came only with achievement, and silence came with mistakes. I learned early that being "good" meant being perfect, quiet, helpful, and never needing anything. So, I buried my emotions, my desires, and even my voice just to feel safe.

But as an adult, that buried part of me started to fight back.

I felt resentful when others didn't notice my efforts. I felt crushed by criticism. I struggled to say no or ask for help. And deep down, I still feared that if I messed up, I'd be abandoned.

That's when I began the work of **reparenting**.

At first, it felt awkward. But slowly, I started showing up for myself the way I needed someone to show up for me back then.

- I began speaking to myself gently when I made a mistake.
- I allowed myself to rest without guilt.
- I gave myself permission to cry and feel, without fixing or shaming.
- I started saying, "You're safe. I'm here. I've got you."

Reparenting didn't mean blaming those who couldn't give me what I needed. It meant **taking responsibility** for how I care for myself now. It meant giving myself the validation, patience, and protection I never had but always deserved.

It's still a daily choice. But every time I choose to respond with love instead of criticism, I rewrite the story. I become both the parent and the protector I once needed. And I finally started to feel whole, not because someone else had completed me, but because I had come **home to myself**.

Connecting to the Inner Child: A Step-by-Step Process

1. **Meet Them**

   Close your eyes. Visualize yourself at age 5, 7, or 9. What do they look like? What are they wearing? Where are they?

2. **Dialogue**

   Ask them: "What do you need from me today?" Let them answer freely. Respond with kindness and curiosity.

249

3. **Soothing**

    Offer comfort. "I see you. I'm here. You're safe with me now." Even if it feels awkward, keep going.

4. **Integration**

    Carry them with you. Let your adult self-guide, but let your inner child inform your joy, play, creativity, and intuition.

1. Reconnecting with the Inner Child

1. What is your earliest memory of feeling safe, joyful, or loved?

    _____

    _____

    _____

    _____

    _____

    _____

    _____

    _____

    _____

2. What did you most need to hear as a child but rarely or never did?

    _____

    _____

    _____

    _____

    _____

    _____

_____

_____

_____

_____

3. What activities or moments made you feel most free,
    creative, or curious?

_____

_____

_____

_____

_____

_____

_____

_____

2. Identifying Childhood Wounds

4. When do you remember feeling misunderstood, invisible,
    or ashamed as a child?

_____

_____

_____

_____

_____

_____

_____

_____

_____

_____

5. Were there times you had to grow up too fast? What was happening then?

_____

_____

_____

_____

_____

_____

_____

_____

6. What emotions were you taught were "bad" or "too much" to express?

_____

_____

_____

_____

_____

_____

_____

_____

_____

3. Current Triggers, Old Roots

7. What situations or people today trigger intense emotional reactions in you?

_____

_____

_____

_____

_____

_____

_____

_____

8. Is there a younger version of you that still feels unprotected, unloved, or not good enough?

_____

_____

_____

_____

_____

_____

_____

_____

9. How do you cope with pain now, and does any of that mirror how you coped as a child?

_____

_____

_____

_____

_____

_____

_____

_____

4. Loving the Inner Child

10. What would your inner child say to you right now if they could speak freely?

_____

_____

_____

_____

_____

_____

_____

_____

_____

11. What does your inner child need from you today?

_____

_____

_____

_____

_____

_____

_____

_____

_____

12. How can you make space for more play, softness, and rest in your adult life?

_____

_____

_____

_____

_____

_____

_____

_____

_____

5. Healing and Reparenting

13. What boundaries, structure, or support would your inner child have thrived under?

_____

_____

_____

_____

_____

_____

_____

_____

14. How can you start offering that structure or emotional safety to yourself now?

_____

_____

_____

_____

_____

_____

_____

_____

15. What does it mean to you to "reparent" yourself with love?

_____

_____

_____

_____

_____

_____

_____

_____

_____

Affirmations for the Inner Child

1. I see you. I hear you. I love you.
2. You are safe now. You don't have to hide.
3. Your feelings matter. I honor your voice.
4. You were never too much. You were always enough.
5. I will protect your light.
6. You don't have to earn love; you are worthy of it.
7. I am the adult I've been waiting for.

Journal Prompts to Reconnect with Your Inner Child

1. What were you most afraid of as a child?

_____

_____

_____

_____

_____

_____

_____

_____

_____

_____

2. What was your favorite way to play? How can you invite
    that joy into your adult life?

    _____

    _____

    _____

    _____

    _____

    _____

    _____

    _____

3. What did you most need to hear that you never heard?

    _____

    _____

    _____

    _____

    _____

    _____

_____

_____

_____

4. When do you still feel "little" in your adult life, and how do you usually respond?

_____

_____

_____

_____

_____

_____

_____

_____

5. If your inner child could write you a letter, what would they say?

_____

_____

_____

_____

_____

_____

_____

_____

Healing Rituals and Practices

Inner Child Letter Writing

Write a letter from your adult self to your child self. Tell them what they never got to hear. Offer them protection, understanding, and unconditional love.

Comfort Object Practice

Place a childhood photo on your altar, mirror, or journal. Greet it each day. Remind your inner child, "You are safe now."

Creative Play

Engage in something playful: finger painting, building something, dancing alone to music you loved as a child. Let your inner child lead without judgment.

The Inner Child as a Source of Magic

While the inner child holds pain, it also holds your imagination, intuition, play, and purity of heart. Healing that child does not just restore safety; it restores magic. It allows you to live more fully, more freely, and more joyfully.

"Your inner child is not just wounded, they are also wise. Let them teach you how to wonder again."

—Inner Mirror Teaching

Dear Little Me,

I see you. I remember how often you felt like you had to be perfect to be loved, how you stayed quiet when you wanted to scream, how you smiled when you wanted to cry. I remember the ache in your chest when people didn't notice your hurt, or when they did and dismissed it anyway.

You were so brave. You didn't know it then, but every time you held in your pain just to survive the moment, you were protecting your heart the only way you knew how. I want you to know that I don't blame you for any of it. You were never too much. You were never not enough. You were just... trying. And that was more than enough.

I'm sorry no one told you that your feelings were valid. That your softness was not a weakness, but a gift. I'm sorry you had to grow up so fast and carry the weight of other people's moods and expectations. You were just a child, and yet you felt responsible for everything.

Today, I'm here with you. You don't have to be strong all the time. You don't have to fix everything or keep the peace. I've got you now. You're safe with me.

When you're scared, I'll hold you. When you're angry, I'll listen. When you want to play, I'll make space for joy. We're healing now, together. This practice of reparenting and integrating the vulnerable parts of the self creates a profound internal sense of safety.

Yet, even when the inner child feels safe, the limiting **rules** they learned in survival often persist, operating like silent agreements deep in the subconscious mind. We must now address the architecture of belief they constructed.

Chapter 13:
Rewriting Limiting Beliefs – Reclaiming the Power of Inner Narrative

"Your beliefs become your thoughts, your thoughts become your words, your words become your actions..."
—Mahatma Gandhi

Introduction: The Architecture of Belief

Every person lives inside an unseen framework of **beliefs**, built from childhood experiences, social conditioning, trauma, and culture. These beliefs shape what we expect, how we perceive the world, and, most importantly, how we perceive and treat ourselves. As Mahatma Gandhi observed, "Your beliefs become your thoughts, your thoughts become your words, your words become your actions... ." To rewrite these limiting beliefs is to become the conscious author of your future.

Some examples:

- *"I have to be perfect to be loved."*
- *"My needs are too much."*
- *"Success always comes at a cost."*
- *"People always leave."*

These internalized narratives live deep within the subconscious mind and often operate beneath awareness, driving patterns of self-sabotage, avoidance, overcompensation, or burnout.

To rewrite them is not to deny your history; it is to become the conscious author of your future.

Where Do Limiting Beliefs Come From?

1. **Family Systems and Childhood Messaging**

   Beliefs like *"I don't matter"* or *"I have to earn love"* often stem from emotionally unavailable or inconsistent caregivers.

2. **Cultural and Societal Norms**

   Gender roles, racial bias, religious dogma, and class-based narratives can restrict identity and self-worth. These scripts are often so normalized they become invisible.

3. **Trauma and Repetition**

   When a painful experience goes unprocessed, especially abuse, betrayal, or neglect, the nervous system encodes a belief to prevent it from happening again. Unfortunately, that belief becomes a cage.

4. **Internalized Authority Figures**

   Harsh teachers, critical parents, and shaming peers; these voices become our inner critic, repeating distorted truths as if they were facts.

Common Limiting Beliefs and Their Transformations

Limiting Belief	Liberating Reframe
"I'm not enough."	"I am already whole."
"I always mess things up."	"I learn and grow from every experience."
"If I speak my truth, I'll be rejected."	"My truth deserves to be heard with love."
"I can't trust anyone."	"I can discern who is safe and trust myself first."
"I'm too much."	"My presence is powerful, not excessive."

Love Meant Doing Everything

There was a time when I believed that love meant doing everything for someone else, even if it meant doing nothing for myself.

That belief wasn't taught in school or handed to me outright. It was modeled, absorbed, and inherited like wallpaper that had been there so long I forgot it wasn't part of the wall itself.

I believed that my role, especially as a mother, was to sacrifice. To carry the weight, keep the peace, meet every need, and ask for nothing in return. And I did it all gladly, desperately, because somewhere deep inside, I thought *this* was what love looked like. That if I gave enough, maybe I'd finally feel like enough.

My son was my heart. Still is. But for a long time, he didn't see me beyond what I could do for him. If I couldn't say yes to something he wanted, it would become, *"You never do anything for me."* If I tried to explain how I felt, it was brushed aside or met with silence. I was pouring out everything I had, and still, somehow, it wasn't enough for him. And worse, my thoughts, my needs, my voice didn't seem to matter.

It broke me in ways I didn't even understand at the time.

I would lie awake at night wondering how he could say those things. I wondered if I had failed him or, worse, failed myself. I was doing everything I could, yet it felt like I didn't exist to him outside of what I could provide. I wasn't being loved. I was being used. And the more I gave, the more invisible I became.

That was the moment I started to see the architecture underneath my life. The unspoken framework supporting all the choices I'd made. The belief that *my worth was tied to how much I could endure.* That *being needed* was the same as *being loved.* That *good mothers never put themselves first.*

And that belief system? It was cracking.

Because I was tired. Not just physically, but spiritually. Tired of not being considered. Tired of believing that loving others meant disappearing myself.

So, I started doing something radical, I started listening to my own voice.

I began asking:

- What do *I* need right now?
- What am I teaching him about love by abandoning myself?
- What if being a good mother isn't about doing everything, but about modeling boundaries and self-respect?

And slowly, I began dismantling the old architecture—brick by brick.

I stopped explaining myself when I said no. I stopped over-functioning just to avoid conflict. I let myself matter. Not loudly or angrily, but consistently.

It wasn't easy. It still isn't. My son didn't transform overnight. He still struggles to see me as a human being with my own limits and needs. But I am no longer waiting for him to validate my worth. I am doing that work myself now.

And what I've discovered is this:

The architecture of belief doesn't crumble in one day. But the moment you begin to question it, the moment you say *enough, that's* when the rebuilding begins.

Now, my home, my internal world, is being redesigned. Not around sacrifice, but mutual respect. Not around being everything for everyone, but being true to myself. And if love can't make room for that, it isn't really love at all.

The Science of Belief and Neuroplasticity

"The brain is shaped by what it repeatedly thinks."
—Dr. Caroline Leaf

Thanks to the science of neuroplasticity, we know that consistent, conscious thought patterns can change beliefs. The brain is not fixed; it is dynamic. When we affirm a new belief, especially when it is paired with emotion, imagery, or repetition, it begins to create new neural pathways.

This means your old beliefs are not your destiny. With practice and patience, you can rewire the way you think, feel, and experience yourself.

The Inner Mirror Process: Rewriting a Limiting Belief

1. **Identify the Belief**

   What belief holds you back the most? Try completing this sentence:

   "I can't ____ because I believe ____."

2. **Trace Its Origins**

   When did you first start believing this? Who or what taught you this? Is it even *yours*?

3. **Challenge Its Authority**

   Is this belief *always* true? Has there ever been a moment when it wasn't?

4. **Name the Cost**

   What has this belief cost you? In love, creativity, health, joy?

5. **Craft a New Core Belief**

   What truth do you want to embody instead? Say it in the present tense: *"I am allowed to take up space."*

6. **Integrate with Emotion and Repetition**

   Use mantras, mirror work, journaling, and visualization to anchor the new belief in your nervous system.

For most of my life, I carried the quiet, heavy belief: "I am not enough."

Not smart enough.

Not pretty enough.

Not talented enough.

Not lovable enough.

I didn't say it out loud, but it showed up in how I lived. I over-explained everything. I worked twice as hard to prove myself. I stayed in relationships that didn't honor me. I settled again and again because some part of me believed that asking for more meant I was ungrateful, or worse, unrealistic.

The first time I tried mirror work, I couldn't even look myself in the eyes. The silence was uncomfortable. The stillness felt threatening. But I stayed. I took a breath. And I whispered:

"Why do I believe I'm not enough?"

What surfaced was a memory I hadn't thought about in years, being in middle school and coming home excited about my grades, only to be met with, "Why didn't you get all A's?" It was never said with cruelty, but the message landed: *Almost isn't enough. You need to earn your worth.*

From that point on, I chased external validation like it was oxygen. And each time I got it, it only filled me for a second, then the emptiness returned.

So, I started the work. Slowly. Gently.

Each day, I stood in front of the mirror and replaced the lie with truth:

"I am enough. Not because of what I achieve. Not because of how I look. But because I exist. Because I breathe. Because I feel. That's enough."

Some days, I believed it. Some days I didn't. But I said it anyway.

And one day, I cried while saying it. Not because I was broken, but because I was finally starting to believe that I never had to be anyone else to be worthy of love.

Now, when I feel the old story creeping in, I return to the mirror. Not to fix myself, but to remember myself. To see the truth behind the mask.

I am enough.

I always have been.

I always will be.

1. Identify the Limiting Belief

1. What belief do you keep coming back to when you feel anxious, rejected, or stuck?

    Complete this sentence: *"Deep down, I believe I am."*

    _____

    _____

    _____

    _____

    _____

_____

_____

_____

_____

_____

2.   Where do you think this belief came from? Can you recall a moment or message that planted the seed?

_____

_____

_____

_____

_____

_____

_____

_____

_____

2. Explore How It Shows Up

4.   How has this belief shaped your relationships, goals, or self-image?

_____

_____

_____

_____

_____

_____

_____

_____

_____

5. What behaviors or habits do you notice when this belief is active (e.g., people-pleasing, perfectionism, isolation)?

_____

_____

_____

_____

_____

_____

_____

_____

3. Challenge the Belief

7. Is this belief *always* true? Can you think of a time it wasn't?

_____

_____

_____

_____

_____

_____

_____

_____

_____

_____

8. Whose voice do you hear when this belief gets loud? Is it really yours?

_____

_____

_____

_____

_____

_____

_____

_____

9. If a friend believed this about themselves, what would you say to them?

_____

_____

_____

_____

_____

_____

_____

_____

4. Rewrite the Belief

10. What is a more compassionate or empowering belief you could replace this with?

_____

_____

_____

_____

_____

_____

_____

_____

5. Integration & Practice

13. What daily actions or affirmations can help you anchor this new belief?

_____

_____

_____

_____

_____

_____

_____

_____

_____

14. What would it look like to live from this new belief—for one hour, one day, one week?

_____

_____

_____

_____

_____

_____

_____

_____

_____

Affirmations for Rewriting Limiting Beliefs

1. I am no longer loyal to my wounds. I am loyal to my growth.
2. I rewrite the story of my life with compassion and courage.
3. My past taught me, but it does not define me.
4. I release beliefs that no longer serve who I am becoming.
5. My worth is not conditional. It is intrinsic and eternal.
6. I have permission to believe in my power and my peace.
7. I create new beliefs that honor my truth, not my fear.
8. I trust the voice of my soul more than the echoes of my past.

Quotes to Anchor This Work

"Beliefs are choices. Choose beliefs that serve your soul."
—Unknown
"Don't believe everything you think."
—Byron Katie

"You are not a prisoner of your past. You are the architect of your future."

—Inner Mirror Teaching

Journal Prompts for Rewriting Limiting Beliefs

1. What belief about yourself feels most painful or limiting right now?

_____

_____

_____

_____

_____

_____

_____

_____

_____

2. Where or from whom did this belief originate?

_____

_____

_____

_____

_____

_____

_____

_____

_____

3. What would your life look like if you no longer believed this?

_____

_____

_____

_____

_____

_____

_____

_____

4. What part of you is still loyal to this belief? Why?

_____

_____

_____

_____

_____

_____

_____

5. What does your soul know to be truer than this belief?

_____

_____

_____

_____

_____

_____

_____

_____

_____

_____

_____

Exercises for Belief Transformation

Core Belief Excavation

List three limiting beliefs. Next to each, write how it affects your daily life. Then, write the opposite as a mantra and practice it for 7 days.

Voice Dialogue

Write a dialogue between the voice of the limiting belief and the voice of your higher self. Let them speak freely. End with your higher self-offering a blessing of truth.

Belief Mapping

Draw a timeline of where a core belief has shown up in your life, relationships, career, and health. Then map a new timeline with your redefined belief.

Conclusion: You Are the Author Now

Your beliefs are not permanent. They are not your identity. They are inherited scripts, and you have the right to revise them.

You are not broken. You are awakening.

To rewrite your beliefs is to return to your original power, the part of you that remembers: *You are not who the world told you to be. You are who your soul knows you are becoming. Having bravely confronted the limiting narratives of the past and the protective programming of your younger self, the work shifts from **excavation to aspiration**.*

Chapter 14:
Mirror Work with Your Future Self

Becoming the Woman, You're Meant to Be, One Reflection at a Time

Mirror work is often discussed as a means of healing the past by looking into our eyes and meeting the wounded child, the unloved teenager, and the silenced adult. But there's another mirror we rarely speak to: The mirror that shows who we are becoming. As the teaching suggests, "The future version of you is already watching, already cheering, already waiting. She's not asking you to be perfect, only to keep becoming". This reflection is not about regret; it's about remembrance.

After the Silence of Abuse, I Found My Voice

Me (Now):

You look free. Unbothered.

How did you escape the version of us that was always afraid?

Me (Becoming):

I didn't escape her; I sat with her.

I held her hand when no one else would.

I whispered prayers into the nights we thought would never end.

And slowly, I chose to believe that we deserved more.

Me (Now):

I still hear his voice.

The one that told me I was too much, too loud, too broken.

How did you silence him?

Me (Becoming):

I didn't.

I just stopped letting his voice be louder than God's.

I turned my ears to the truth: that I am loved, chosen, worthy.

And I started speaking to myself with kindness, until his words lost their power.

Me (Now):

I feel ashamed. For staying so long.

For losing myself. For not knowing how to leave.

Me (Becoming):

But you *did* leave.

You crawled your way out of the darkness, even when you couldn't see the path.

You weren't weak; you were surviving.

And every step since has been a testimony of strength.

Me (Now):

Will I ever trust again?

Will I ever feel safe in my own body?

Me (Becoming):

Yes.

You'll learn to trust the rhythm of your breath.

You'll choose peace over chaos.

You'll make a home inside yourself, where no one can steal your light again.

Me (Now):

What gave you the courage?

Me (Becoming):

Remember that night you fell to your knees and asked for help?

That was the beginning.

When you stopped reaching for control and reached for your Higher Source.

That was when heaven met you in your wreckage.

And from there, you rose.

Me (Now):

I don't know who I am anymore.

Me (Becoming):

You're becoming someone new.

Not because the old you was unworthy but because she was never allowed to thrive.

Now, you are free to create a life that reflects your truth, not your trauma.

So take your time.

Healing is not linear.

But every boundary, every prayer, every moment of choosing yourself—

It is a step toward *me*.

And I promise you…

I'm worth the journey.

Who Is Your Future Self?

Let's get honest. You already know who they are.
Even if you don't know the full details, you've felt the whisper.

It is the version of you who:

- Walks away when peace is too expensive to buy with your self-worth.
- Speaks your boundaries and still smiles afterwards.
- No longer chooses crumbs just because she's afraid to be alone.
- Believes in *divine timing* instead of deadlines created by fear.
- Holds herself with compassion when she falls.
- Laughs again, deep belly laughs that don't apologize for joy.

What She Has That You Don't (Yet)

The only thing separating you from her is *your belief that that person is far away*.

But it is actually not.

In every small, brave decision you make:

- Every time you pause before reacting
- Every time you go to therapy or journal through your resistance
- Every time you take the longer road of growth over the shorter path of comfort

- Every time you say, *"I deserve more than this"* and mean it

You don't need to be perfect. You need to **not quit**.

Personal Mirror Work Prompts (And My Answers)

Here's how I've learned to use mirror work to embody my future self, not just dream about her.

Prompt: What do I admire about the future version of me?

She moves with calm. She trusts herself. She no longer needs to prove her worth to anyone.

Prompt: What does she no longer tolerate?

She walks away from chaos without needing to justify it. She doesn't chase, she chooses.

Prompt: What choices is she making daily?

She nourishes herself. She protects her energy. She wakes up and asks, "What would love do today?"

Prompt: How does she talk to herself in the mirror?

She looks into her eyes and says, "You've come so far. I'm proud of you. Keep going."

Try this for 5–10 minutes a day:

1. **Stand in front of the mirror.**
   Don't fix your hair. Don't judge your face. Just look.

2. **Imagine your highest self is looking back.**
   Not a perfect self. But a grounded, healed, whole self. What are you wearing? What is your posture? What energy surrounds you?

3. **Speak directly to yourself.**
   Start with:
   "I see you."
   "Thank you for holding space for me."
   "I'm doing the work. I'm coming for you."
   "Teach me how to move like you."
   "I love the woman I'm becoming."

4. **Ask yourself for guidance.**
   Let her respond, not from your head, but from your heart. Write it down. Sit with it.

279

5. **Close with a mantra.**
   Something like: *"Every version of me that I've been is worthy. But the person I'm becoming is sacred."*

"She's not waiting for a perfect moment.

She's becoming in the middle of the mess.

She's not becoming someone else.

She's finally becoming herself."

Who Is Your Future Self?

Your future self is not a distant stranger waiting for you somewhere down the road.

She is already here, waiting patiently inside you, quietly growing through the cracks left by pain and struggle.

As the poet Rumi beautifully said, *"The wound is the place where the light enters you."*

Your future self is the light emerging from those very wounds.

She is the one who no longer lets the past define her worth.

She is the voice inside that whispers, *"I am enough. I am safe. I am free."*

Her strength does not come from perfection, but from courage, the courage to face her scars, to lean into vulnerability, and to embrace every part of her story.

She has learned to dance with her scars, rather than hiding them.

She understands, as Brené Brown reminds us, *"Owning our story and loving ourselves through that process is the bravest thing that we'll ever do."*

Her healing isn't about forgetting; it's about reclaiming your story and rewriting it with compassion, truth, and grace.

Your future self holds hands with courage and vulnerability, walking forward with a fierce softness.

She embraces imperfection not as failure but as evidence of growth and resilience.

Every morning, she wakes up with the intention of choosing boundaries, peace, and joy over fear and self-doubt.

She knows the power in saying *"no"* when something doesn't serve her and *"yes"* when it nurtures her soul.

She is fiercely compassionate toward herself and others, practicing kindness as a revolutionary act.

Your future self is the woman who looks back at you in the mirror, standing tall, not because she is perfect, but because she is real and complete.

She is the survivor who learned to thrive, the once-broken now made whole, the shadow transformed into light.

As Maya Angelou said, *"You may not control all the events that happen to you, but you can decide not to be reduced by them."*

Your future self-embodies that fierce refusal to be diminished.

Ask yourself:

What does she look like?

How does she speak to you?

What choices is she making today to become who she is meant to be?

Is she gentle with her heart?

Is she setting boundaries that protect her peace?

Is she speaking her truth with kindness and strength?

Your future self is calling you to keep going, one brave step at a time.

She is the sacred promise of transformation, waiting for you to say yes to the journey.

As the writer Audre Lorde said, *"I am deliberate and afraid of nothing."*

Your future self is deliberate. She is fearless.

She is ready.

All you have to do is trust her.

Mirror Work with My Future Self

For most of my life, I avoided mirrors.

They weren't just glass; they were truth-tellers, and I wasn't ready for the truth.

When I did look, I didn't just see a face. I saw a history.

The curve of my mouth carried the weight of silenced words.

My eyes were tired. Watchful told stories of a little girl who learned early that love came with conditions, that survival meant swallowing feelings, smiling when she wanted to cry, and nodding along when someone else rewrote her memories.

Neglect taught me to survive on leftovers, leftover attention, leftover approval, leftover safety.

Gaslighting taught me to question my own mind until I didn't trust my own heartbeat.

People-pleasing wasn't a habit; it was my lifeline.

And then there was my shine.

A light so bright inside me, it couldn't help but spill out, though most didn't see it that way.

They saw my brightness as too much, too loud, too intense, too different and instead of seeing the real me behind the light, they pushed me away, judged me, or tried to dim what made me who I am.
It was easier for them to paint me in shadows than to face their own discomfort with someone who dared to glow.

But one night, everything shifted.

It was late. The kind of late where the world is quiet, but your mind is screaming. I couldn't sleep; the anxiety had crept into my chest like it always did. I got up to get water, but as I passed the bathroom, I caught a glimpse of myself. Normally, I would've looked away. But something made me stop.

I stepped closer. My face in the mirror looked… tired, yes, but there was something else.

And then I felt this strange, steady presence.

It was me. But not the me who survived by disappearing. This was the me I'd been trying to remember. The me I'd been fighting to find. My future self.

She didn't rush to speak. She just looked at me with this unshakable calm, as if to say, *"I know everything you've been through. I was there. And still — here we are."*

Her eyes told me I wasn't broken, just bruised. That I wasn't too sensitive, too much, or hard to love. That I wasn't imagining the harm done to me happened, and it mattered. And still… I mattered more.

From that night on, mirror work wasn't about forcing myself to say pretty affirmations. It was about meeting her.

Every time I stood there, I practiced being who she already knew I was.

When someone tried to guilt me into saying yes, I'd remember her steady gaze and choose no.

When old shame bubbled up, I'd place my hand on the mirror and remind myself, *"We're not living in that story anymore."*

When the anxiety came at 2 a.m., I'd look into the glass and whisper, *"You're safe now."*

And slowly, I began to see it not just in the mirror, but in my life.

In the grocery store, I permitted myself to take up space in the aisle.

On the phone, when I calmly said, "That doesn't work for me."

Even in moments of silence, when I let myself breathe without waiting for permission.

Now, when I stand in front of the mirror, I don't just see the girl who was gaslit, neglected, and misunderstood.

I see a woman who walked through fire and carried her own ashes into a new life.

I see the face of someone who chose herself, finally, fully and never looked back.

Journal Prompts

1. Who is your future self, and what would it feel like to honor her now?

_____

_____

_____

_____

_____

_____

_____

_____

_____

_____

2. What would you have to release in order to meet her fully?

_____

_____

_____

_____

_____

_____

_____

_____

3. What limiting beliefs or habits would she no longer
    entertain?

_____

_____

_____

_____

_____

_____

_____

_____

4. How does she rest? How does she protect her joy?

_____

_____

_____

_____

_____

_____

_____

_____

_____

5. How can your daily choices reflect where you're headed, not where you've been?

_____

_____

_____

_____

_____

_____

_____

_____

_____

Closing Invitation:

The mirror is no longer your enemy. It's your mentor. And your future self? She's already loving you through the becoming. Your task is to act accordingly, embodying the truth that "I already am everything I hope to be."

Yet, when you step into your stronger, freer self, you may find that the internal work of healing meets external friction.

Chapter 15:
When Your Light Shines Too Bright

Growth is a beautiful thing. It means you are evolving, shedding old layers, and stepping into a stronger, freer version of yourself. But growth also comes with a challenge. The more you rise, the more you may notice that not everyone around you is celebrating with you. Sometimes, the more you shine, the more others feel threatened, uncomfortable, or resentful. This is not a reflection of your worth. It reflects their readiness, or unreadiness, to face their own shadows.

Why Your Growth Feels Threatening to Others

You've journeyed through your shadows, reclaimed your inner child, set sacred boundaries, and rewritten your core story. That deep work changed the way you see yourself. Now, it's time to realize that this immense internal shift creates an unavoidable external friction. The outside world—relationships, family dynamics, friendships—will act as a final, unsparing mirror to the depth of your healing. Chapter 4 discussed how *others* reflect *your* unhealed wounds; this chapter examines how your healing reflects *their* unaddressed pain.

When your light shines too bright, it isn't an attack on your worth; it's a reflection of their readiness to face their own shadows. Your courage awakens their fear. Your authenticity highlights their compliance. Your presence reveals their avoidance. This final mirror shows you definitively who in your life is prepared to rise with you, and whose loyalty was tied to the person you once were

Personal Story: Outgrowing the Old Version

That moment wasn't a sudden, dramatic explosion, but a quiet, irreversible implosion of the persona I had worn for years. The "old version" of me was built on a foundation of shoulds: I should be quieter, I should prioritize his comfort, I should accept the life we had engineered, and it began to crumble during a drive home from yet another dinner where I had laughed at a joke that felt dismissive of my own career. I caught my reflection in the dark car window, and for a split second, I didn't recognize the woman staring back. Her eyes were tired, her smile practiced, and her spirit seemed to occupy only a fraction of her own body. The realization hit like a physical pressure: this comfortable, accommodating wife was a character I was desperately tired of playing, and my marriage was merely the stage upon which she performed. When I finally walked out the door weeks later, it wasn't the sound of a failure leaving, but the decisive click of a cage door opening, allowing the real me to finally breathe and inhabit the space I had made for her.

The Hidden Dynamics of Change

Growth exposes relationships. Friends, family, and even your partner might start feeling uncomfortable with the new you. They may not understand why you've stopped putting up with certain things, why you now say no instead of always agreeing, or why you're suddenly setting boundaries that never used to be there.

Instead of seeing your healing as a positive transformation, some may resist it. They may try to pull you back into old versions of yourself because that feels safer for them. They may even label your changes as selfishness, arrogance, or rebellion when, in truth, you are simply choosing authenticity over approval.

Signs People Feel Threatened by Your Light

Sometimes the signs are obvious. Other times they are subtle. Pay attention when people:

1. Dismiss your progress or minimize your achievements, acting as if they are not worthy of acknowledgment.
2. Criticize you more often, especially when you express joy, confidence, or independence.
3. Bring up your past mistakes, not to support your growth, but to keep you tied to a version of yourself you have already outgrown.
4. Withdraw, block communication, or avoid you instead of engaging with the person you are becoming.
5. Call you selfish, full of yourself, or accuse you of changing, as though change were something shameful.
6. Gossip about you when they used to celebrate you.
7. Compete with you instead of supporting you, turning everything into a comparison game.

288

Personal Story: Friendship Shift

A friend of mine once told me, "You're different now. You're too focused on yourself." At first, her words cut deeply. This was someone I had leaned on for years, someone I thought would be proud of me for healing. But I realized what she really meant was, "You're not the same person who used to make me feel better about staying stuck."

She wanted the old version of me who kept herself small so she could feel comfortable. When I stopped venting endlessly and started celebrating my progress, she couldn't relate to me anymore. It hurt to let that friendship fade, but it also reminded me: the right people don't see your growth as a threat. They see it as inspiration.

The Truth About Your Light

Your growth is not meant to make others comfortable. It is meant to make you whole. You are not responsible for shrinking yourself so others can stay the same. You are not responsible for dimming your glow so that others can avoid facing their shadows.

If someone feels threatened by your progress, it is often because they recognize in you what they have yet to allow themselves to become. Your courage awakens their fear. Your healing highlights their wounds. Your expansion contrasts with their resistance.

And yet, this does not mean you should stop. Quite the opposite. Your light is needed more than ever.

How to Handle It with Grace

When others react negatively to your growth, it can be tempting to shrink back. But you do not need to apologize for shining. Instead, you can respond with grace and power.

Stay grounded in your truth. Remember why you began this journey. Write down your reasons for choosing growth and keep them close when doubt creeps in. Your purpose is not to win approval but to honor your soul.

Communicate clearly and calmly. When someone questions your changes, you do not need to defend yourself with anger. A calm "This is important to me" or "I am choosing what feels right for me now" can be more powerful than a long explanation. Your clarity speaks louder than their criticism.

Hold boundaries firmly but kindly. Boundaries are not punishments. They are expressions of self-respect. You can say no without guilt and walk away without apology. Protecting your peace is an act of love for yourself and, indirectly, for those who truly care about you.

Release the need for approval. Not everyone will cheer for you, and that is okay. Some people will fall away as you grow. Instead of clinging to their acceptance, trust that the right people, those aligned with your light, will remain and rise with you.

Surround yourself with supportive voices. Find communities, friendships, or mentors who celebrate your growth. Being in the company of people who uplift you will remind you that your light is not only welcome but necessary.

Keep shining anyway. Your light is not meant to be hidden. Even if others try to dim it, even if they misunderstand you, keep growing, keep healing, and keep shining. The right people will not only accept your radiance but will be inspired by it.

Personal Story: Choosing to Shine Anyway

I once had a coworker who constantly belittled my ideas in meetings. Every time I spoke up, he would interrupt, make a joke, or dismiss my perspective. For a while, I stayed quiet to avoid embarrassment. But then I realized my silence was giving him power.

The next time he tried to cut me off, I calmly said, "I'd like to finish my thought." My voice was steady, even though my heart was pounding. That moment changed everything. He never had to like my voice, but I refused to let him silence it. I kept shining anyway. And over time, others began speaking up too.

Closing Reflection

The world does not need you to wear a mask. It does not need you to pretend. It needs the raw, authentic, radiant version of you. When you shine, you give permission for others to shine too, even if at first they resist or recoil.

You do not apologize for growing. Do not shrink for comfort. Keep shining, keep expanding, and keep walking boldly in your truth. ...

Empowering Affirmation Today, I choose to shine without apology. I no longer dim my light for the comfort of others.

I am light. I am love. I am free

Empowering Affirmation

Today, I choose to shine without apology.
I no longer dim my light for the comfort of others.
My growth is sacred. My truth is powerful.
I release the need for approval and embrace authenticity.
I am light. I am love. I am free.

Chapter 16:
Becoming the Embodiment of Your Healing

There comes a moment on the healing path when insight is no longer enough. You've journaled. You've cried. You've whispered mantras and stared into the mirror. As James Clear reminds us, "You do not rise to the level of your goals. You fall to the level of your systems." This chapter is about moving beyond intellectual knowing and into the living, daily systems of embodiment. It's time to live the healing.

Insight Isn't the Destination—Embodiment Is

For years, I thought having a breakthrough meant I was done. *"I finally understand why I people-please!"* I'd declare. Then I'd get invited to a family event, feel obligated, and say yes out of guilt, only to end up feeling drained and resentful. The truth is that healing is not a linear process, and it's not just about intellectual understanding alone. As Andrew Bennett once said, *"The longest journey you will ever take is the 18 inches from your head to your heart."*

Healing is about rewiring the nervous system. *"Your nervous system is not your enemy—it is your protector. Teach it safety, and it will learn peace."* It's about new behaviors. It's about practice. *"What you practice, you become."* Every small choice is a thread in the fabric of who you're becoming.

You might have heard the phrase, *"The body keeps the score."* The body also retains the memory of healing. Each time you choose differently, opting for truth over performance, boundaries over guilt, and love over fear, you embody a new truth. *"Healing is not about becoming someone new, but about becoming who you were meant to be before the world taught you fear."* You show your nervous system a new way to be safe. You shift the default setting. And with every act of courage and self-respect, you echo the truth: *"Every act of self-care is a declaration: 'I am worth my own time and energy.'"*

Here are some signs that you're beginning to live the work:

- You notice your triggers, but they don't own you.
- You pause instead of react.
- You listen to your intuition, even when it's inconvenient.
- You say "no" without explaining yourself.
- You show yourself grace on bad days instead of self-punishment.
- You become more interested in your peace than in being understood.

Becoming the Embodiment of My Healing

The true measure of my healing wasn't when I stopped crying, but when I finally permitted myself to embrace color again. For fifteen years across two marriages, my world had been subtly muted: safe, beige walls, practical clothing, and hobbies that fit neatly into the masculine space of the garage or the televised schedule of a sports game. I had mistakenly equated being a good partner with being small and unobtrusive. The moment of awakening arrived when I unpacked an old set of acrylic paints, a gift from college that had been relegated to a damp box since my first wedding. I set up a makeshift studio in the corner of my new, single-occupancy living room. I didn't paint anything meaningful; I simply played. The smell of the turpentine, the vibrant streak of cadmium yellow, and the thick, satisfying texture of the paint knife against the canvas felt like a profound physical reconnection to the person I had abandoned. It was the first time in years I made something that had no purpose other than the sheer, unadulterated joy of its creation. I realized that the life I was building now was not merely stable or acceptable; it was rich, textured, and unapologetically mine, and this joyful self-expression was the clearest, most vibrant proof that I had healed and fully embodied my own freedom.

Becoming the embodiment of your healing means:

- Showing up as your *whole* self, even when you're still tender.
- Rooting into your values, not your wounds.

- Making peace more familiar than chaos.
- Choosing love over fear, one conversation, one boundary, one breath at a time.

I'm still healing. I always will be. But now, it's not something I'm trying to prove.

It's something I carry in my posture. My tone. My relationships. My rest.

Because healing isn't something I perform.

It's who I've become.

Morning Mirror Ritual

Stand in front of the mirror. Hand over your heart. Say out loud:

"I honor who I was. I embrace who I am. I welcome who I'm becoming."

Let your eyes soften. Breathe into your belly. Anchor your presence in your body.

The Body As Teacher

Each day, check in:

What is my body feeling? What does it need?

Sometimes, healing is as simple as drinking more water, stretching, or allowing for rest. **You don't abandon yourself to perform worthiness anymore.**

Speak the Language of the Healed You

When your inner critic gets loud, reply out loud:

"That's not how we talk to ourselves anymore."

You are rewiring. Every time you say, "We don't shrink to stay safe," your body starts to believe it.

Journal Prompts

1. When did I most recently *embody* the version of me I've been working to become?

_____

_____

_____

_____

_____

_____

_____

_____

_____

2. What small habit no longer aligns with who I am
   becoming?

_____

_____

_____

_____

_____

_____

_____

_____

3. What do my thoughts sound like when I feel most
   grounded?

_____

_____

_____

_____

_____

_____

_____

_____

4. What does safety in my body feel like, and how can I
    return to it more often?

_____

_____

_____

_____

_____

_____

_____

_____

_____

5. What would it look like to make peace feel more familiar
    than pain?

_____

_____

_____

_____

_____

_____

_____

_____

You may not always feel healed, but you are becoming the evidence of your healing.

In the way you show up for yourself.

In this way, you stop chasing closure from people who refuse to grow.

In the way you honor your intuition.

In the way you love, not from desperation, but from abundance.

This chapter of your life doesn't need to be loud. Let it be steady. Let it be embodied. Let it be real.

Don't rush to prove it to anyone.

Live it.

Walk it.

Let your energy speak louder than your words.

And when life invites you to react to old wounds, smile gently and say:

"I don't live there anymore."

Embracing the Mirror — Your Ongoing Journey

As you reach the end of this book, pause for a moment and honor yourself for the bravery it took to embark on this journey. Engaging in mirror work invites vulnerability, honesty, and courage into your life. It is to say "yes" to seeing yourself fully, your light and shadow, your strengths and wounds, your beauty and your brokenness.

The mirror you have held up before your soul is far more than a simple reflection of your face. It is a sacred portal into your inner world, a gateway where your stories live, your fears whisper, and your truth waits to be embraced. In gazing into this mirror, you have faced what many shy away from: the complexity of your own humanity.

Perhaps you met resistance. Perhaps you encountered pain and discomfort that felt unbearable at times. This is the nature of deep healing: it asks us to walk through the fire, not around it. As Rumi wrote, *"Try to accept the changing seasons of your heart, even as you have always accepted the changing seasons passing over the fields."* And yet, through this challenge, you have also found grace, clarity, and profound connection with the woman you are and the woman you are becoming.

297

Healing is not a destination or a fixed state. It is a sacred, ongoing process of becoming. Like a river flowing toward the sea, you move in cycles and spirals, sometimes gentle, sometimes wild, always evolving. On some days, you may feel strong, radiant, and unstoppable. On other days, you may feel tired, fragile, or unsure. As Brené Brown reminds us, *"Owning our story and loving ourselves through that process is the bravest thing that we will ever do."* All of these moments are part of your unfolding, and all are worthy of your compassion.

Through mirror work, you have defied the stories that once bound you—the voices that told you that you were not enough, not worthy, or not lovable. This work is a revolutionary act of self-love, a reclaiming of your power to choose how you see yourself. As Louise Hay, the pioneer of mirror work, once said, *"Remember, you have been criticizing yourself for years, and it hasn't worked. Try approving yourself and see what happens."* You are rewriting the narratives of limitation and opening the door to radical self-acceptance, forgiveness, and love.

But this book is not the end of your story. It is the beginning. It is a call to continue the sacred dance with your soul, a lifelong commitment to return to the mirror, again and again, with kindness and curiosity. *"The journey isn't about becoming a different person; it's about loving who you are right now,"* whispers the mirror. And as you step forward, may you remember the words of Maya Angelou: *"You alone are enough. You have nothing to prove to anybody."*

As you continue your journey, remember these enduring truths:

- You are inherently worthy of love and kindness—not because of what you do or how you look, but because you exist.

- Your scars, visible or hidden, are not signs of weakness or shame, but emblems of your resilience and courage.

- Every part of you, the inner child, the shadow, the light, is sacred and deserving of respect and care.

- The boundaries you set, the self-care you practice, and the joy you claim are acts of radical self-honoring.

- You are never alone. The divine, the universe, your higher self, and countless ancestors walk beside you, offering strength and grace.

The mirror in front of you is more than glass; it is a living testament to your journey. It reflects your past struggles and pain, but also your courage in healing and transforming. It shows you not only who you are today but who you are becoming: a woman reborn through love and grace.

Step forward gently. Step forward boldly. Step forward with trust in the unfolding mystery of your life.

Keep returning to the mirror with patience and openness. Keep honoring every feeling, every story, every moment of growth. Keep listening to the quiet voice within that whispers, *"I see you. I believe you. I will never leave you."*

This promise, this sacred covenant, is yours to carry. It binds you to your own healing, to your own truth, and to the divine presence that guides you.

You are a sacred work in progress, complex, beautiful, evolving. And the mirror will always be here, reflecting the depths of your soul and the radiant light you hold within.

Walk forward with grace.

Walk forward with love.

Walk forward knowing you are enough, just as you are and infinitely worthy of the life you dream of.

Your journey is your own holy pilgrimage.

May it be filled with healing, hope, and the ever-present embrace of your true self.

Final Reflection:
The Light You Were Born to Shine

There comes a time in life when we must stop apologizing for who we are and start reclaiming the parts of ourselves we once abandoned for acceptance.

"Owning our story and loving ourselves through that process is the bravest thing that we'll ever do."

— Brené Brown

Too many people carry invisible wounds, subtle, inherited beliefs that whisper: *"You're not good enough."* These beliefs seep into our choices, convincing us to settle for jobs that stifle our purpose or relationships that drain our spirit. They convince us to shrink, to dim our light, to trade our dreams for comfort or approval.

"You're playing small does not serve the world."

— Marianne Williamson

Each time we stay silent instead of speaking, choose fear instead of growth, or live by duty instead of truth, we move further away from who we really are. Mirror work invites us to pause and look closely, to see how much we've been carrying that was never truly ours.

One of the most heartbreaking things I've witnessed, both in others and within myself, is how often people settle. We settle for jobs that drain us, for relationships that deplete us, for routines that numb us. We justify it in the name of practicality, responsibility, or "being realistic."

"Don't trade your authenticity for approval."

— Unknown

Underneath those layers of logic is often a deeper wound: the belief that we are not good enough to ask for more. That we don't deserve the dream, the love, the joy we long for. And so we shrink.

"You either walk inside your story and own it, or you stand outside your story and hustle for your worthiness."

— Brené Brown

Every time we say "yes" to something that dims our light, we are, sometimes quietly, sometimes violently, saying "no" to the life we were meant to live.

Mirror work invites you to turn toward the parts of yourself you've avoided. To look at the parts that believed you were unworthy and ask them, *"Who told you that?"* And more importantly, *"Why did I believe them?"*

This is not an easy process. Looking in the mirror means confronting the very stories that have defined your life and often realizing they were never yours to begin with.

When we finally see ourselves clearly, not through the distorted lens of other people's opinions or past pain, but through the eyes of truth, we begin to remember who we are. We remember that we are light. That we are power. That we are enough not because of what we do, but because of who we are.

"No one can make you feel inferior without your consent."
— Eleanor Roosevelt

In that remembering, we begin to choose differently. We leave jobs that suffocate us and step into work that feeds our souls. We stop begging for love and begin embodying it. We no longer tolerate crumbs when we were born for the feast.

"Do not settle for less just because it's available."

— Unknown

We stop performing for approval and start living from authenticity. We take up space. We speak our truth. We become the mirror others didn't know they needed.

But this transformation takes courage. Courage to let go of identities rooted in survival. Courage to disappoint others to be true to yourself. Courage to believe in a version of you that no one else may understand yet.

"She was never quite ready, but she was brave. And the universe listens to brave."

— Rebecca Ray

Let me remind you: Your dreams are not random. Your vision is not selfish. Your light is not too much. The life you desire is a divine echo of the person you were always meant to become.

"The only permission, the only validation, and the only opinion that matters in our quest for greatness is our own."

— Steve Maraboli

You do not have to shrink to be accepted. You do not have to earn your worth. You do not have to carry shame that isn't yours. The world doesn't need a watered-down version of you; it needs you. Fully. Boldly. Unapologetically.

So if no one told you today: You are enough. You are worthy. You are loved. And you are allowed to want more.

As you close this book, I invite you to look in the mirror, really look. Not at your flaws or your failures, but at the fire in your eyes. The strength in your scars. The beauty in your becoming.

"And one day she discovered that she was fierce, and strong, and full of fire, and that not even she could hold herself back because her passion burned brighter than her fears."

— Mark Anthony

You didn't come this far just to settle. You came to rise.

Now go live like it.

www.ingramcontent.com/pod-product-compliance
Lightning Source LLC
Chambersburg PA
CBHW070908130626
46555CB00001B/46